CS-11   GENERAL APTITUDE AND ABILITIES SERIES

This is your
PASSBOOK for...

Graphs, Charts and Tables (Tabular Material)

Test Preparation Study Guide
Questions & Answers

COPYRIGHT NOTICE

This book is SOLELY intended for, is sold ONLY to, and its use is RESTRICTED to individual, bona fide applicants or candidates who qualify by virtue of having seriously filed applications for appropriate license, certificate, professional and/or promotional advancement, higher school matriculation, scholarship, or other legitimate requirements of education and/or governmental authorities.

This book is NOT intended for use, class instruction, tutoring, training, duplication, copying, reprinting, excerption, or adaptation, etc., by:

1) Other publishers
2) Proprietors and/or Instructors of "Coaching" and/or Preparatory Courses
3) Personnel and/or Training Divisions of commercial, industrial, and governmental organizations
4) Schools, colleges, or universities and/or their departments and staffs, including teachers and other personnel
5) Testing Agencies or Bureaus
6) Study groups which seek by the purchase of a single volume to copy and/or duplicate and/or adapt this material for use by the group as a whole without having purchased individual volumes for each of the members of the group
7) Et al.

Such persons would be in violation of appropriate Federal and State statutes.

PROVISION OF LICENSING AGREEMENTS – Recognized educational, commercial, industrial, and governmental institutions and organizations, and others legitimately engaged in educational pursuits, including training, testing, and measurement activities, may address request for a licensing agreement to the copyright owners, who will determine whether, and under what conditions, including fees and charges, the materials in this book may be used them. In other words, a licensing facility exists for the legitimate use of the material in this book on other than an individual basis. However, it is asseverated and affirmed here that the material in this book CANNOT be used without the receipt of the express permission of such a licensing agreement from the Publishers. Inquiries re licensing should be addressed to the company, attention rights and permissions department.

All rights reserved, including the right of reproduction in whole or in part, in any form or by any means, electronic or mechanical, including photocopying, recording, or by any information storage and retrieval system, without permission in writing from the Publisher.

Copyright © 2024 by
National Learning Corporation

212 Michael Drive, Syosset, NY 11791
(516) 921-8888 • www.passbooks.com
E-mail: info@passbooks.com

PASSBOOK® SERIES

THE *PASSBOOK® SERIES* has been created to prepare applicants and candidates for the ultimate academic battlefield – the examination room.

At some time in our lives, each and every one of us may be required to take an examination – for validation, matriculation, admission, qualification, registration, certification, or licensure.

Based on the assumption that every applicant or candidate has met the basic formal educational standards, has taken the required number of courses, and read the necessary texts, the *PASSBOOK® SERIES* furnishes the one special preparation which may assure passing with confidence, instead of failing with insecurity. Examination questions – together with answers – are furnished as the basic vehicle for study so that the mysteries of the examination and its compounding difficulties may be eliminated or diminished by a sure method.

This book is meant to help you pass your examination provided that you qualify and are serious in your objective.

The entire field is reviewed through the huge store of content information which is succinctly presented through a provocative and challenging approach – the question-and-answer method.

A climate of success is established by furnishing the correct answers at the end of each test.

You soon learn to recognize types of questions, forms of questions, and patterns of questioning. You may even begin to anticipate expected outcomes.

You perceive that many questions are repeated or adapted so that you can gain acute insights, which may enable you to score many sure points.

You learn how to confront new questions, or types of questions, and to attack them confidently and work out the correct answers.

You note objectives and emphases, and recognize pitfalls and dangers, so that you may make positive educational adjustments.

Moreover, you are kept fully informed in relation to new concepts, methods, practices, and directions in the field.

You discover that you are actually taking the examination all the time: you are preparing for the examination by "taking" an examination, not by reading extraneous and/or supererogatory textbooks.

In short, this PASSBOOK®, used directedly, should be an important factor in helping you to pass your test.

Sample Test Material for:
Understanding and interpreting tabular material

Test material will be presented in a multiple-choice question format.

Test Task: The questions in this subject area are contained in two or more sets. Each set consists of data presented in one or more tables, followed by a number of questions. Candidates must use the appropriate data from the table, in combination with the information given in each question, in order to answer the questions correctly.

SAMPLE TABLE:

Directions: Base your answers to the following three questions on the information in the table below.

Population of a City by Age and Gender
(In Thousands)

Age	Female	Male	Total
Under 25	70	72	142
25-34	?	27	?
35-44	?	28	53
45-54	27	28	55
55-64	30	?	57
65 and over	85	75	160
Total	261	257	518

Note: Spaces with question marks can be filled in using information given in the table and in the questions.

SAMPLE QUESTION 1:

How many people in the city were between 25 and 34 years old?

A. 51
B. 27,000
C. 51,000
D. cannot be determined from the information provided

The correct answer to sample question 1 is Choice C.

Solution:

To answer this question correctly, you must first note that the numbers in the table represent thousands of people (see the table heading). You are asked to find the total number of people aged 25-34. Since this information is missing from the table, it is necessary to calculate it by using other information which is in the table. You must add the number of people in all the age groups other than 25-34, and then subtract this sum from the total population of the city. This will then give the number of people aged 25-34.

```
142,000      under 25
+53,000      35-44              518,000   total population (all ages)
+55,000      45-54             - 467,000  total population (all ages except 25-34)
+57,000      55-64               51,000   population aged 25-34
+160,000     65 and over
467,000
```

There are 51,000 people in the city between the ages of 25 and 34 (choice C).

SAMPLE QUESTION 2:

Most nearly, what percent of the total population of the city was female aged 35 to 54?

A. 5%
B. 10%
C. 14%
D. 20%

The correct answer to sample question 2 is Choice B.

Solution:

To answer this question correctly you must find the number of females aged 35 to 54. This requires you to add the number of females aged 35-44 to the number aged 45-54. You must first find the number of females who are aged 35 to 44. This information is missing from the table, but you can calculate it by subtracting the number of males who are aged 35 to 44 from the total number of people in that age group.

(53,000 – 28,000 = 25,000; there are 25,000 females aged 35-44).

You then need to add the number of females aged 35-44 to the number of females aged 45-54; (25,000 + 27,000 = 52,000; there are 52,000 females between the ages of 35 and 54).

You must then divide this number by the total population of the city, and convert the answer to a percent. (52,000/518,000 = .100386; **this is nearest to 10%**).

Therefore, the percentage of the total population of the city which was female aged 35 to 54 is 10% (choice B).

SAMPLE QUESTION 3:

If 40% of the total male population of the city earns wages, and 30% of the total female population of the city earns wages, which one of the following statements comparing the number of males earning wages to the number of females earning wages is true?

A. There are 24,500 more males than females earning wages.
B. There are 27,300 more males than females earning wages.
C. There are 51,800 more males than females earning wages.
D. There are 27,300 fewer males than females earning wages.

The correct answer to sample question 3 is Choice A.

Solution:

To answer this question correctly you must use some information given in the question and some information given in the table. It is important to be careful and apply the correct percentage for each gender. (The percentage for males is given first in the question, but the number of males is second in the table).

To calculate the number of males earning wages, multiply the total number of males by 40%.
(257,000 x .40 = 102,800)

To calculate the number of females earning wages, multiply the total number of females by 30%.
(261,000 x .30 = 78,300)

To compare the two numbers, subtract the number of female wage earners from the number of male wage earners.
(102,800 – 78,300 = 24,500)

There are 24,500 more male wage earners than female wage earners (choice A).

HOW TO TAKE A TEST

You have studied long, hard and conscientiously.

With your official admission card in hand, and your heart pounding, you have been admitted to the examination room.

You note that there are several hundred other applicants in the examination room waiting to take the same test.

They all appear to be equally well prepared.

You know that nothing but your best effort will suffice. The "moment of truth" is at hand: you now have to demonstrate objectively, in writing, your knowledge of content and your understanding of subject matter.

You are fighting the most important battle of your life—to pass and/or score high on an examination which will determine your career and provide the economic basis for your livelihood.

What extra, special things should you know and should you do in taking the examination?

I. YOU MUST PASS AN EXAMINATION

A. WHAT EVERY CANDIDATE SHOULD KNOW
Examination applicants often ask us for help in preparing for the written test. What can I study in advance? What kinds of questions will be asked? How will the test be given? How will the papers be graded?

B. HOW ARE EXAMS DEVELOPED?
Examinations are carefully written by trained technicians who are specialists in the field known as "psychological measurement," in consultation with recognized authorities in the field of work that the test will cover. These experts recommend the subject matter areas or skills to be tested; only those knowledges or skills important to your success on the job are included. The most reliable books and source materials available are used as references. Together, the experts and technicians judge the difficulty level of the questions.
Test technicians know how to phrase questions so that the problem is clearly stated. Their ethics do not permit "trick" or "catch" questions. Questions may have been tried out on sample groups, or subjected to statistical analysis, to determine their usefulness.
Written tests are often used in combination with performance tests, ratings of training and experience, and oral interviews. All of these measures combine to form the best-known means of finding the right person for the right job.

II. HOW TO PASS THE WRITTEN TEST

A. BASIC STEPS

1) Study the announcement

How, then, can you know what subjects to study? Our best answer is: "Learn as much as possible about the class of positions for which you've applied." The exam will test the knowledge, skills and abilities needed to do the work.

Your most valuable source of information about the position you want is the official exam announcement. This announcement lists the training and experience qualifications. Check these standards and apply only if you come reasonably close to meeting them. Many jurisdictions preview the written test in the exam announcement by including a section called "Knowledge and Abilities Required," "Scope of the Examination," or some similar heading. Here you will find out specifically what fields will be tested.

2) Choose appropriate study materials

If the position for which you are applying is technical or advanced, you will read more advanced, specialized material. If you are already familiar with the basic principles of your field, elementary textbooks would waste your time. Concentrate on advanced textbooks and technical periodicals. Think through the concepts and review difficult problems in your field.

These are all general sources. You can get more ideas on your own initiative, following these leads. For example, training manuals and publications of the government agency which employs workers in your field can be useful, particularly for technical and professional positions. A letter or visit to the government department involved may result in more specific study suggestions, and certainly will provide you with a more definite idea of the exact nature of the position you are seeking.

3) Study this book!

III. KINDS OF TESTS

Tests are used for purposes other than measuring knowledge and ability to perform specified duties. For some positions, it is equally important to test ability to make adjustments to new situations or to profit from training. In others, basic mental abilities not dependent on information are essential. Questions which test these things may not appear as pertinent to the duties of the position as those which test for knowledge and information. Yet they are often highly important parts of a fair examination. For very general questions, it is almost impossible to help you direct your study efforts. What we can do is to point out some of the more common of these general abilities needed in public service positions and describe some typical questions.

1) General information

Broad, general information has been found useful for predicting job success in some kinds of work. This is tested in a variety of ways, from vocabulary lists to questions about current events. Basic background in some field of work, such as sociology or economics, may be sampled in a group of questions. Often these are principles which have become familiar to most persons through exposure rather than through formal training. It is difficult to advise you how to study for these questions; being alert to the world around you is our best suggestion.

2) Verbal ability
An example of an ability needed in many positions is verbal or language ability. Verbal ability is, in brief, the ability to use and understand words. Vocabulary and grammar tests are typical measures of this ability. Reading comprehension or paragraph interpretation questions are common in many kinds of civil service tests. You are given a paragraph of written material and asked to find its central meaning.

IV. KINDS OF QUESTIONS

1. Multiple-choice Questions
Most popular of the short-answer questions is the "multiple choice" or "best answer" question. It can be used, for example, to test for factual knowledge, ability to solve problems or judgment in meeting situations found at work.

A multiple-choice question is normally one of three types:
- It can begin with an incomplete statement followed by several possible endings. You are to find the one ending which best completes the statement, although some of the others may not be entirely wrong.
- It can also be a complete statement in the form of a question which is answered by choosing one of the statements listed.
- It can be in the form of a problem – again you select the best answer.

Here is an example of a multiple-choice question with a discussion which should give you some clues as to the method for choosing the right answer:

When an employee has a complaint about his assignment, the action which will best help him overcome his difficulty is to
    A. discuss his difficulty with his coworkers
    B. take the problem to the head of the organization
    C. take the problem to the person who gave him the assignment
    D. say nothing to anyone about his complaint

In answering this question, you should study each of the choices to find which is best. Consider choice "A" – Certainly an employee may discuss his complaint with fellow employees, but no change or improvement can result, and the complaint remains unresolved. Choice "B" is a poor choice since the head of the organization probably does not know what assignment you have been given, and taking your problem to him is known as "going over the head" of the supervisor. The supervisor, or person who made the assignment, is the person who can clarify it or correct any injustice. Choice "C" is, therefore, correct. To say nothing, as in choice "D," is unwise. Supervisors have and interest in knowing the problems employees are facing, and the employee is seeking a solution to his problem.

2. True/False

3. Matching Questions
Matching an answer from a column of choices within another column.

V. RECORDING YOUR ANSWERS

Computer terminals are used more and more today for many different kinds of exams.

For an examination with very few applicants, you may be told to record your answers in the test booklet itself. Separate answer sheets are much more common. If this separate answer sheet is to be scored by machine – and this is often the case – it is highly important that you mark your answers correctly in order to get credit.

VI. BEFORE THE TEST

YOUR PHYSICAL CONDITION IS IMPORTANT

If you are not well, you can't do your best work on tests. If you are half asleep, you can't do your best either. Here are some tips:

1) Get about the same amount of sleep you usually get. Don't stay up all night before the test, either partying or worrying—DON'T DO IT!
2) If you wear glasses, be sure to wear them when you go to take the test. This goes for hearing aids, too.
3) If you have any physical problems that may keep you from doing your best, be sure to tell the person giving the test. If you are sick or in poor health, you relay cannot do your best on any test. You can always come back and take the test some other time.

Common sense will help you find procedures to follow to get ready for an examination. Too many of us, however, overlook these sensible measures. Indeed, nervousness and fatigue have been found to be the most serious reasons why applicants fail to do their best on civil service tests. Here is a list of reminders:

- Begin your preparation early – Don't wait until the last minute to go scurrying around for books and materials or to find out what the position is all about.
- Prepare continuously – An hour a night for a week is better than an all-night cram session. This has been definitely established. What is more, a night a week for a month will return better dividends than crowding your study into a shorter period of time.
- Locate the place of the exam – You have been sent a notice telling you when and where to report for the examination. If the location is in a different town or otherwise unfamiliar to you, it would be well to inquire the best route and learn something about the building.
- Relax the night before the test – Allow your mind to rest. Do not study at all that night. Plan some mild recreation or diversion; then go to bed early and get a good night's sleep.
- Get up early enough to make a leisurely trip to the place for the test – This way unforeseen events, traffic snarls, unfamiliar buildings, etc. will not upset you.
- Dress comfortably – A written test is not a fashion show. You will be known by number and not by name, so wear something comfortable.
- Leave excess paraphernalia at home – Shopping bags and odd bundles will get in your way. You need bring only the items mentioned in the official notice you received; usually everything you need is provided. Do not bring reference books to the exam. They will only confuse those last minutes and be taken away from you when in the test room.

- Arrive somewhat ahead of time – If because of transportation schedules you must get there very early, bring a newspaper or magazine to take your mind off yourself while waiting.
- Locate the examination room – When you have found the proper room, you will be directed to the seat or part of the room where you will sit. Sometimes you are given a sheet of instructions to read while you are waiting. Do not fill out any forms until you are told to do so; just read them and be prepared.
- Relax and prepare to listen to the instructions
- If you have any physical problem that may keep you from doing your best, be sure to tell the test administrator. If you are sick or in poor health, you really cannot do your best on the exam. You can come back and take the test some other time.

VII. AT THE TEST

The day of the test is here and you have the test booklet in your hand. The temptation to get going is very strong. Caution! There is more to success than knowing the right answers. You must know how to identify your papers and understand variations in the type of short-answer question used in this particular examination. Follow these suggestions for maximum results from your efforts:

1) Cooperate with the monitor

The test administrator has a duty to create a situation in which you can be as much at ease as possible. He will give instructions, tell you when to begin, check to see that you are marking your answer sheet correctly, and so on. He is not there to guard you, although he will see that your competitors do not take unfair advantage. He wants to help you do your best.

2) Listen to all instructions

Don't jump the gun! Wait until you understand all directions. In most civil service tests you get more time than you need to answer the questions. So don't be in a hurry. Read each word of instructions until you clearly understand the meaning. Study the examples, listen to all announcements and follow directions. Ask questions if you do not understand what to do.

3) Identify your papers

Civil service exams are usually identified by number only. You will be assigned a number; you must not put your name on your test papers. Be sure to copy your number correctly. Since more than one exam may be given, copy your exact examination title.

4) Plan your time

Unless you are told that a test is a "speed" or "rate of work" test, speed itself is usually not important. Time enough to answer all the questions will be provided, but this does not mean that you have all day. An overall time limit has been set. Divide the total time (in minutes) by the number of questions to determine the approximate time you have for each question.

5) Do not linger over difficult questions

If you come across a difficult question, mark it with a paper clip (useful to have along) and come back to it when you have been through the booklet. One caution if you do this – be sure to skip a number on your answer sheet as well. Check often to be sure that you have not lost your place and that you are marking in the row numbered the same as the question you are answering.

6) Read the questions

Be sure you know what the question asks! Many capable people are unsuccessful because they failed to read the questions correctly.

7) Answer all questions

Unless you have been instructed that a penalty will be deducted for incorrect answers, it is better to guess than to omit a question.

8) Speed tests

It is often better NOT to guess on speed tests. It has been found that on timed tests people are tempted to spend the last few seconds before time is called in marking answers at random – without even reading them – in the hope of picking up a few extra points. To discourage this practice, the instructions may warn you that your score will be "corrected" for guessing. That is, a penalty will be applied. The incorrect answers will be deducted from the correct ones, or some other penalty formula will be used.

9) Review your answers

If you finish before time is called, go back to the questions you guessed or omitted to give them further thought. Review other answers if you have time.

10) Return your test materials

If you are ready to leave before others have finished or time is called, take ALL your materials to the monitor and leave quietly. Never take any test material with you. The monitor can discover whose papers are not complete, and taking a test booklet may be grounds for disqualification.

VIII. EXAMINATION TECHNIQUES

1) Read the general instructions carefully. These are usually printed on the first page of the exam booklet. As a rule, these instructions refer to the timing of the examination; the fact that you should not start work until the signal and must stop work at a signal, etc. If there are any special instructions, such as a choice of questions to be answered, make sure that you note this instruction carefully.

2) When you are ready to start work on the examination, that is as soon as the signal has been given, read the instructions to each question booklet, underline any key words or phrases, such as least, best, outline, describe and the like. In this way you will tend to answer as requested rather than discover on reviewing your paper that you listed without describing, that you selected the worst choice rather than the best choice, etc.

3) If the examination is of the objective or multiple-choice type – that is, each question will also give a series of possible answers: A, B, C or D, and you are called upon to select the best answer and write the letter next to that answer on your answer paper – it is advisable to start answering each question in turn. There may be anywhere from 50 to 100 such questions in the three or four hours allotted and you can see how much time would be taken if you read through all the questions before beginning to answer any. Furthermore, if you

come across a question or group of questions which you know would be difficult to answer, it would undoubtedly affect your handling of all the other questions.

4) If the examination is of the essay type and contains but a few questions, it is a moot point as to whether you should read all the questions before starting to answer any one. Of course, if you are given a choice – say five out of seven and the like – then it is essential to read all the questions so you can eliminate the two that are most difficult. If, however, you are asked to answer all the questions, there may be danger in trying to answer the easiest one first because you may find that you will spend too much time on it. The best technique is to answer the first question, then proceed to the second, etc.

5) Time your answers. Before the exam begins, write down the time it started, then add the time allowed for the examination and write down the time it must be completed, then divide the time available somewhat as follows:
   - If 3-1/2 hours are allowed, that would be 210 minutes. If you have 80 objective-type questions, that would be an average of 2-1/2 minutes per question. Allow yourself no more than 2 minutes per question, or a total of 160 minutes, which will permit about 50 minutes to review.
   - If for the time allotment of 210 minutes there are 7 essay questions to answer, that would average about 30 minutes a question. Give yourself only 25 minutes per question so that you have about 35 minutes to review.

6) The most important instruction is to read each question and make sure you know what is wanted. The second most important instruction is to time yourself properly so that you answer every question. The third most important instruction is to answer every question. Guess if you have to but include something for each question. Remember that you will receive no credit for a blank and will probably receive some credit if you write something in answer to an essay question. If you guess a letter – say "B" for a multiple-choice question – you may have guessed right. If you leave a blank as an answer to a multiple-choice question, the examiners may respect your feelings but it will not add a point to your score. Some exams may penalize you for wrong answers, so in such cases only, you may not want to guess unless you have some basis for your answer.

7) Suggestions
   a. Objective-type questions
      1. Examine the question booklet for proper sequence of pages and questions
      2. Read all instructions carefully
      3. Skip any question which seems too difficult; return to it after all other questions have been answered
      4. Apportion your time properly; do not spend too much time on any single question or group of questions
      5. Note and underline key words – all, most, fewest, least, best, worst, same, opposite, etc.
      6. Pay particular attention to negatives
      7. Note unusual option, e.g., unduly long, short, complex, different or similar in content to the body of the question
      8. Observe the use of "hedging" words – probably, may, most likely, etc.

9. Make sure that your answer is put next to the same number as the question
10. Do not second-guess unless you have good reason to believe the second answer is definitely more correct
11. Cross out original answer if you decide another answer is more accurate; do not erase until you are ready to hand your paper in
12. Answer all questions; guess unless instructed otherwise
13. Leave time for review

b. Essay questions
1. Read each question carefully
2. Determine exactly what is wanted. Underline key words or phrases.
3. Decide on outline or paragraph answer
4. Include many different points and elements unless asked to develop any one or two points or elements
5. Show impartiality by giving pros and cons unless directed to select one side only
6. Make and write down any assumptions you find necessary to answer the questions
7. Watch your English, grammar, punctuation and choice of words
8. Time your answers; don't crowd material

8) Answering the essay question

Most essay questions can be answered by framing the specific response around several key words or ideas. Here are a few such key words or ideas:

M's: manpower, materials, methods, money, management
P's: purpose, program, policy, plan, procedure, practice, problems, pitfalls, personnel, public relations

a. Six basic steps in handling problems:
1. Preliminary plan and background development
2. Collect information, data and facts
3. Analyze and interpret information, data and facts
4. Analyze and develop solutions as well as make recommendations
5. Prepare report and sell recommendations
6. Install recommendations and follow up effectiveness

b. Pitfalls to avoid
1. Taking things for granted – A statement of the situation does not necessarily imply that each of the elements is necessarily true; for example, a complaint may be invalid and biased so that all that can be taken for granted is that a complaint has been registered
2. Considering only one side of a situation – Wherever possible, indicate several alternatives and then point out the reasons you selected the best one
3. Failing to indicate follow up – Whenever your answer indicates action on your part, make certain that you will take proper follow-up action to see how successful your recommendations, procedures or actions turn out to be
4. Taking too long in answering any single question – Remember to time your answers properly

EXAMINATION SECTION

INTERPRETING STATISTICAL DATA
GRAPHS, CHARTS AND TABLES

Graphs, charts, and tables help us to visualize and to understand more readily ideas that might otherwise be more difficult to grasp.

The language of pictures is one of the oldest and easiest to understand.

There are several types of graphs.

The *pictograph* is used to compare numerical quantities. Symbols or pictures are used to represent numbers. Each symbol or picture represents a certain number of the quantities being compared.

The *bar graph* is employed to emphasize comparisons between numbers. If the graph is constructed of vertical bars, it is called a *vertical bar graph*. A fundamental part of this graph is the scale, which must begin with zero (0). In addition, a title heads this type of graph.

A *horizontal bar graph* employs horizontal bars. Here, too, the scale begins with zero (0), and there is a title

The *line graph* shows how a quantity, such as prices, sales, temperature, rises or falls or changes. This type of graph is particularly good for delineating when the quantity is increasing and when it is decreasing. It also strikingly reveals trends or situations.

The *circle graph* is also used to show comparisons, particularly the relationship between a whole thing and a part of the thing. The whole thing is represented by the circle, which is divided into pieces, called sectors, by the drawing of radii which form central angles. In order to find the number of degrees in the central angle of each sector, the method is to ascertain the fraction of the whole which the sector represents and to multiply by 360°.

Charts and tables also are used to visualize and to concretize facts and figures, to lead to comparisons, and to draw conclusions. Careful reading of the directions given with the charts or tables and of the questions employed in connection therewith, make these visual devices clear and meaningful as the student or candidate learns to be precise and resourceful in his reading and interpretation.

The tests with questions that follow are intended to guide the candidate into the amazing world of graphs, charts, and tables and to point up the importance of the quantitative ability to interpret statistical data.

TEST 1

DIRECTIONS: The following graph represents the national debt of the United States from the year 1991 through the year 2000. From this graph, determine the answers to Questions 1 through 8.

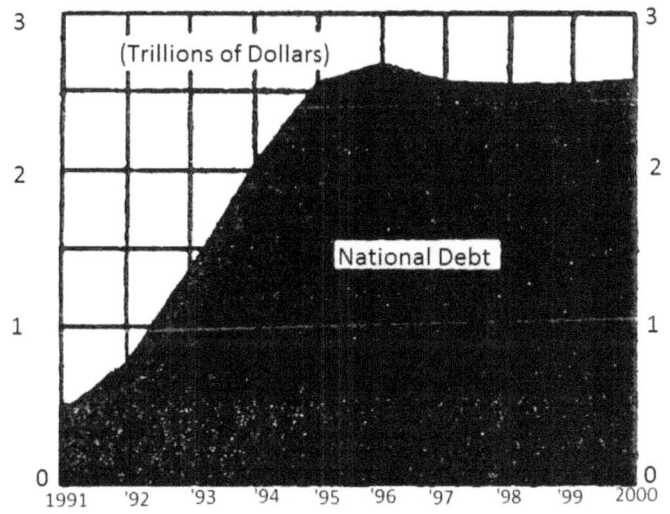

1. How many years are represented by the graph? 1.____

2. In what year was our national debt the smallest? 2.____

3. What was the national debt in 1994? 3.____

4. What was the approximate increase in the national debt from 1993 to 1994? 4.____

5. In what year was our national debt the largest? 5.____

6. In what year did the national debt begin to decrease? 6.____

7. How much greater was the national debt in 2000 than it was in 1991? 7.____

8. In what two consecutive years was the national debt the same? 8i.____

2 (#1)

KEY (CORRECT ANSWERS)

1. 10 (1991 through 2000)

2. 1991 (slightly below .50 trillions of dollars as indicated on the graph)

3. 2 trillion dollars (the line graph for the year 1994 touches exactly on the 2 trillion dollar mark)

4. Approximately .60-.65 trillion dollars (2 trillion dollars in 1994 minus approximately .13 to .14 trillions in 1993)

5. 1996 (approximately .26 trillion dollars)

6. 1996 (the line graph begins to decline starting in this year)

7. Approximately 5 times greater (national debt in 2000, approximately .25 trillion dollars; national debt in 1991, approximately .50 trillion dollars)

8. 1998, 1999 (the line graph does not change for these years)

TEST 2

DIRECTIONS: The following pictogram represents the number of telephones in use in a certain city. Each complete symbol represents 20,000 telephones.

1. How many telephones were in use in this city in 1985? 1._____

2. How many more telephones were in use in this city in 1985 than in 1975? 2._____

3. Find the percent of increase in the number of telephones in use in 1990 over the number in use in 1970. 3._____

4. If it is estimated that 280,000 telephones will be in use in 1995, how many symbols should be used to picture this on the graph? 4._____

2 (#2)

KEY (CORRECT ANSWERS)

1. 220,000 (20,000 × 11 = 220,000)

2. 50,000 (20,000 × 2½)

3. 25% or 25
   (Each symbol = 20,000
   2½ symbols = 50,000
   $\frac{50,000}{200,000}$ (1970 has 10 symbols = ¼ or 25%)

4. 14 (280,000 ÷ 20,000)

TEST 3

DIRECTIONS: The following graph shows the noon temperature at a certain weather station on seven consecutive days in June.

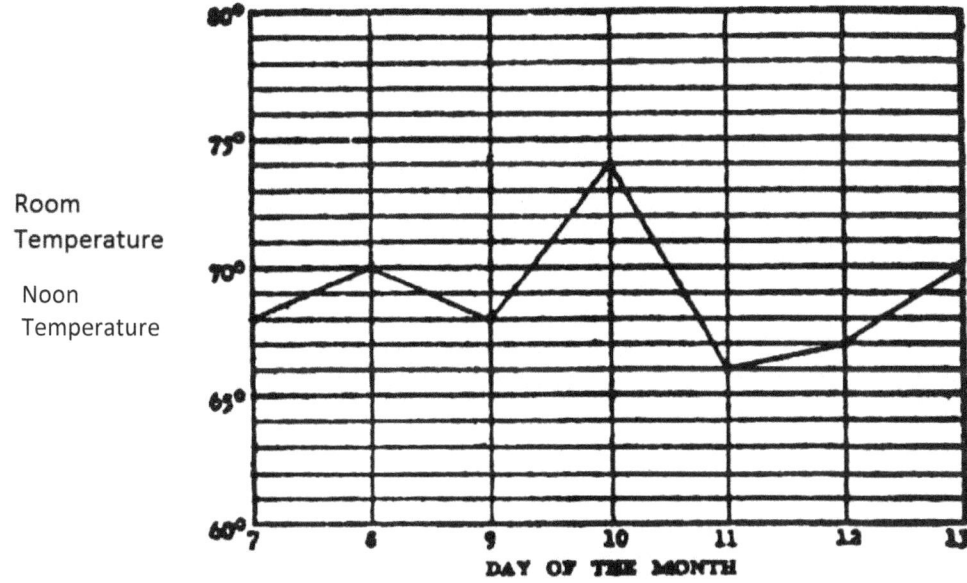

1. On what day was the noon temperature the highest? 1._____

2. For what two consecutive days was the change in noon temperature the least? 2._____

3. For what two consecutive days was the change in noon temperature the greatest? 3._____

4. What was the average noon temperature for the week? 4._____

5. How many degrees warmer was it at noon on June 9 than at noon on June 12? 5._____

2 (#3)

KEY (CORRECT ANSWERS)

1. 10th (74°)

2. 11th and the 12th (on these days the temperature rose from 66° to 67°, a change of 1°)

3. The 10th and the 11th (as shown by the steepest line, when the temperature fell from 74° to 66°, a change of 8°)

4. 69° (adding the temperatures from June 7th to June 13th, we get 483; dividing by 7, we find the average to be 69°)

5. 1° (noon temperature, June 9th: 69°; noon temperature, June 12th: 67°)

TEST 4

DIRECTIONS: The following graph shows food expenditures in the United States for each of the years 1970 to 1990, inclusive.

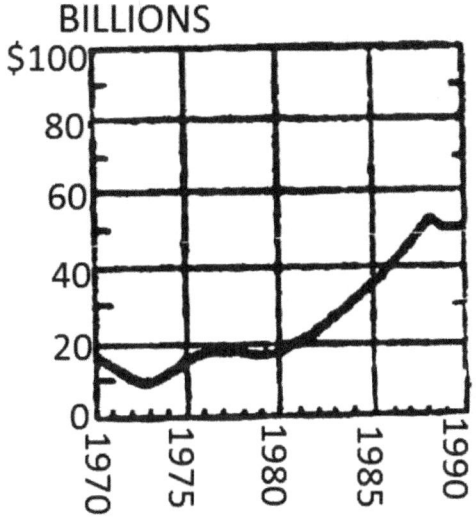

1. During what year were expenditures for food the lowest? 1.____

2. During what year were expenditures for food the highest? 2.____

3. Approximately how many billions of dollars were spent for food in 1990? 3.____

4. In what year did expenditures for food first reach 40 billion? 4.____

5. During which one of these five-year periods (1970-75, 1975-80, 1980-85, 1985-1990) did expenditures for food remain about the same? 5.____

2 (#4)

KEY (CORRECT ANSWERS)

1. 1973 (low point of about 8 billion dollars in this year)

2. 1988 (high point of about 52 billion dollars in this year

3. 50 (approximately 50 billion dollars)

4. 1986 (graph crosses the 40 billion dollar line in this year)

5. 1975-80 (graph line relatively stable for this period)

TEST 5

DIRECTIONS: In a recent year, a large industrial concern used each dollar of its sales income as shown in the following graph.

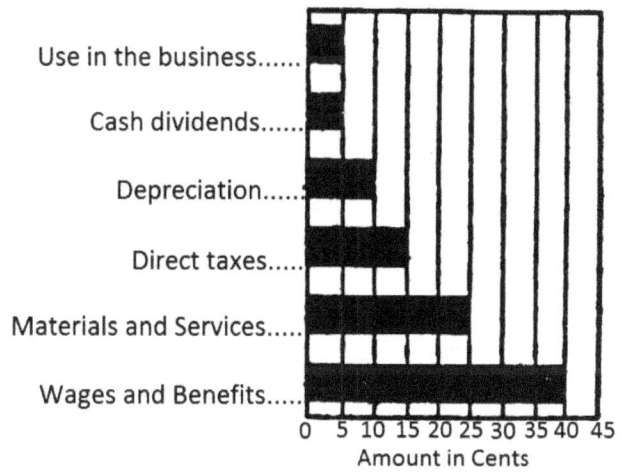

1. How many cents of each dollar of sales income did the company use to pay wages and benefits? 1.____

2. How many more cents out of each sales dollar was spent on wages and benefits than on materials and services? 2.____

3. What was the total number of cents out of each sales dollar that the company set aside for depreciation and for use in the business? 3.____

4. The amount the company paid in direct taxes was how many times the amount it paid in cash dividends? 4.____

5. What percent of each sales dollar was paid in cash dividends? 5.____

2 (#5)

KEY (CORRECT ANSWERS)

1. 40 (the bottom bar which represents wages and benefits, reaches the 40-cent line.

2. 15 (40, representing wages and benefits, minus 25, representing materials and services)

3. 15 (0, representing depreciation, plus 5, representing use in the business)

4. 3 (15 represents direct taxes and 5 represents cash dividends, a ratio of 3 to 1

5. $5 \left(\frac{5}{100}\right) = 5\%$

TEST 6

DIRECTIONS: The following circle graph shows how the wage earners in a certain city earned their living in a recent year. The number of degrees required for each angle is given on the graph.

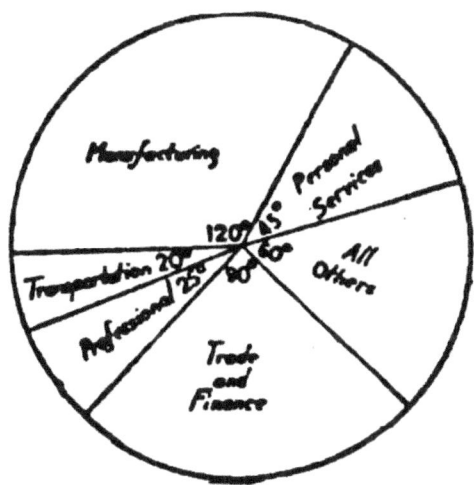

1. Using the number of degrees shown on this graph, find the fractional part of the graph that represents the number of wage earners earning their living in each of the following:
   a. Trade and finance
   b. Personal services
   c. Manufacturing

2. How many times as many persons worked in the area of trade and finance as in the area of personal services?

3. If there were 180,000 wage earners in the city that year, how many persons were engaged in transportation?

1.____

2.____

3.____

KEY (CORRECT ANSWERS)

1. ¼ ($\frac{90°}{360°}$ = ¼)

2. ⅛ ($\frac{80°}{360°}$ = ⅛)

3. ⅓ ($\frac{120°}{360°}$ = ⅓)

4. 2 ($\frac{90°}{45°}$ = 2)

5. 10,000 ($\frac{20°}{360°}$ × 180,000)

———

TEST 7

DIRECTIONS: The following graph shows the relation between car speed and tire wear. The graph appeared in a magazine advertisement.

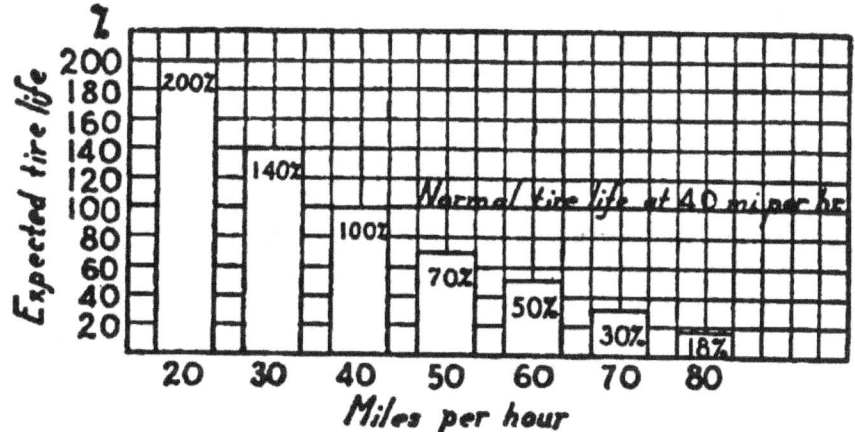

1. At what speed is the normal life of a tire determined? 1.____

2. The life of a tire on a car driven at 20 miles per hour is how many times greater than the life of a tire on a car driven at 40 miles per hour? 2.____

3. What car speed will result in tires lasting only half of their normal tire life? 3.____

4. If a car is driven at 30 miles per hour, what percent more than normal tire life may be expected? 4.____

5. If a car is driven at 70 miles per hour, what percent less than normal tire life may be expected? 5.____

2 (#7)

KEY (CORRECT ANSWERS)

1. 40 miles per hour (as stated in the graph proper)

2. 2 (at 20 miles per hour: expected tire life, 200%; at 40 miles per hour: expected tire life, 100%)

3. 60 miles per hour (as indicated on the graph)

4. 40% (as stated in the graph. 140% or 40% more than normal tire life (100%)

5. 70% (at 70 miles per hour: expected tire life, 30%; this is 70% less than normal tire life (100%)

TEST 8

DIRECTIONS: The following graphs were published by the federal government to show where the tax dollar comes from and where it goes.

WHERE THE TAX DOLLAR COMES FROM

- Corporation income taxes: 31¢
- Borrowing: 4¢
- Excise Taxes: 16¢
- Customs & Other Taxes: 6¢
- Individual income taxes: 43¢

WHERE THE TAX DOLLAR GOES

- Cost of National Security: 68¢
- Costs fixed by law: 22¢
- Cost of Other Government Operations: 10¢

1. What percent of the federal tax dollar was spent on national security? 1.____

2. What percent more money was obtained from individual income taxes than from corporation income taxes? 2.____

3. How many dollars, of every million dollars collected in taxes, were obtained from excise taxes? 3.____

4. List the four sources of income whose total approximately equals the amount spent for national security? 4.____

2 (#8)

KEY (CORRECT ANSWERS)

1. 68% ($\frac{68}{100}$ = 68%)

2. 12% (43 – 31 = 12d on each dollar or 12%)

3. 160,000 (1,000,000 × .16 = 180,000)

4. Borrowing, excise taxes, customs, and other taxes, individual income taxes (.04 + .16 + .06 + .43 = .69 (cost of national security, .68))

TEST 9

DIRECTIONS: A savings bank in a large city published the following graph for its depositors. use the graph to answer Questions 1 through 4.

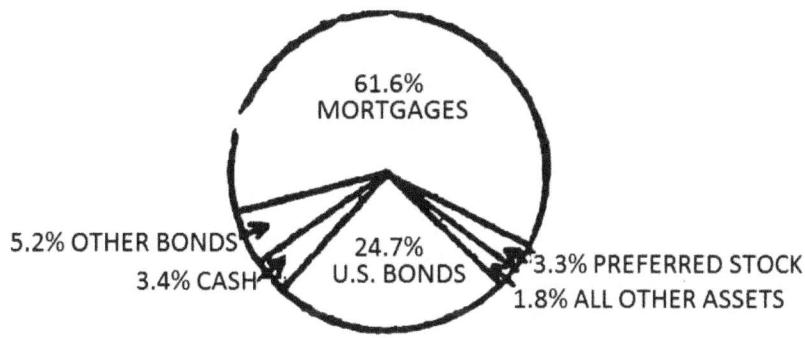

HOW YOUR SAVINGS WORK FOR YOU

1. In what way is approximately one-fourth of the bank's assets invested? 1.____

2. Which fraction is nearest to the bank's total investment in mortgages: ½, ¾, ⁵/₈? 2.____

3. The bank's total assets are $162,575,800. Of this total, what amount is kept in cash? 3.____

4. Approximately how many times as much money is invested in United States Bonds as in other bonds? 4.____

2 (#9)

KEY (CORRECT ANSWERS)

1. U.S Bonds (24.7%)

2. $5/8$ (61.6% is close to 62.5% or $5/8$)

3. $5,527,577.20 (162,575,800 × 3.4% or .034)

4. 5 (approximately 25% - 5 ÷ approximately 5%)

TEST 10

DIRECTIONS: The following graph appeared in a recent publication.

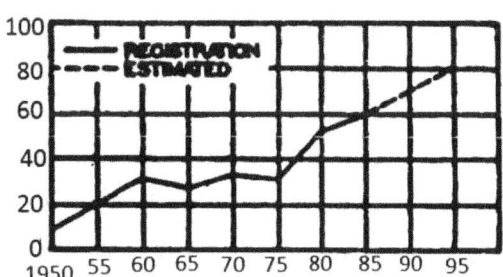

GROWTH IN MOTOR VEHICLE REGISTRATION SINCE 1950

MOTOR VEHICLES REGISTERED IN MILLIONS

1. Approximately how many motor vehicles were registered in 1985? 1.____

2. Approximately how many times as many motor vehicles were registered in 1985 as in 1955? 2.____

3. According to the estimate made on this graph, how many more motor vehicles will be registered in 1995 than in 1985? 3.____

4. What percent of increase in registration is expected between 1985 and 1995? 4.____

2 (#10)

KEY (CORRECT ANSWERS)

1. 60 million (as indicated on the graph as registered)

2. 3 (60 ÷ 20)

3. 20 million (80 million – 60 million)

4. $33^1/_3$ ($\frac{29 \text{ million}}{60 \text{ million}}$ = $^1/_3$ = $33^1/_3$%)

TEST 11

DIRECTIONS: Questions 1 through 5 are based on the following graphs. On the line at the right of each of these statements or questions, write the letter preceding the word or expression that BEST completes the statement or answers the question.

WHAT WE SEND LATIN AMERICA AS A PERCENT OF OUR TOTAL EXPORTS

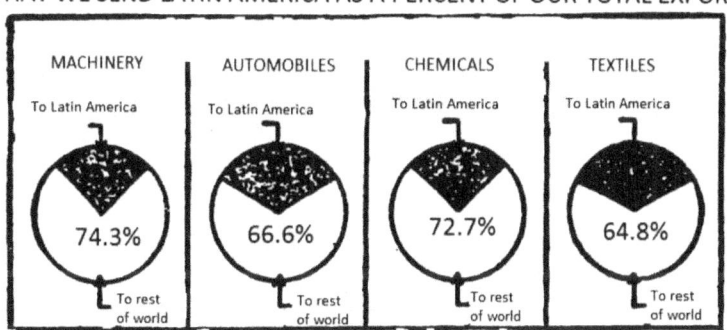

WHAT LATIN AMERICA SENDS US AS A PERCENT OF OUR TOTAL IMPORTS

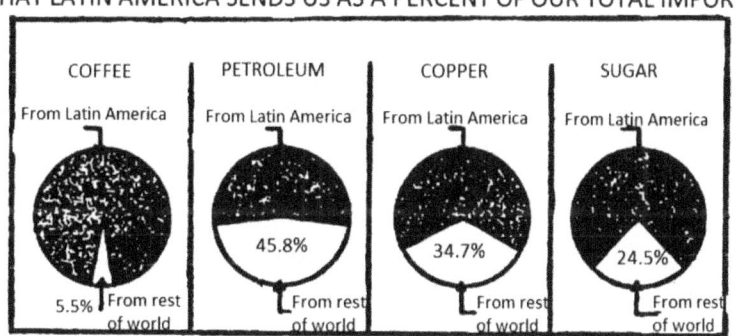

1. The GREATEST export of the United States to Latin America is
   A. automobiles   B. chemicals   C. machinery   D. textiles

   1.____

2. Latin America's GREATEST export to the United States is
   A. coffee   B. sugar   C. copper   D. petroleum

   2.____

3. Products exported by the United States to Latin America are CHIEFLY
   A. agricultural   B. manufactured
   C. mineral   D. forest

   3.____

4. As compared with Latin America's export trade to the United States, the export trade of the United States to Latin America is
   A. greater   B. a little less
   C. about the same   D. much less

   4.____

5. Which statement concerning the foreign trade of the United States is TRUE?
   A. Most of our chemical exports go to areas other than Latin America.
   B. Most of our automobile exports go to Latin America.
   C. Most of our petroleum imports come from areas other than Latin America.
   D. All of our coffee imports come from Latin America.

   5.____

KEY (CORRECT ANSWERS)

1. D
2. A
3. B
4. D
5. A

TEST 12

DIRECTIONS: Last winter in a certain school, Grades 2, 3, 4, 5, and 6 decided to get together supplies to send to needy children in other parts of the world. The total amount collected was 720 pounds.

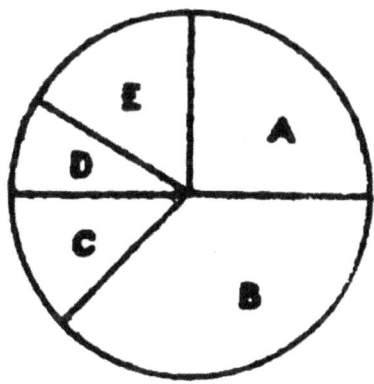

1. The above table shows the number of pounds collected by each grade. Complete the table by writing for each grade the letter that indicates on the graph the fractional part of the total that was collected by that grade.
    a. Grade 2: 180 pounds =
    b. Grade 3: 90 pounds =
    c. Grade 4: 120 pounds =
    d. Grade 5: 60 pounds =
    e. Grade 6: 270 pounds =

    1a.____
    1b.____
    1c.____
    1d.____
    1e.____

2. How many degrees are there in each section of the circle, A, B, C, D, and E?

    2A.____
    2B.____
    2C.____
    2D.____
    2E.____

2 (#12)

KEY (CORRECT ANSWERS)

1.
   a. 180 pounds – A (second largest angle in the circle)
   b. 90 pounds – C (fourth largest angle in the circle)
   c. 120 pounds – E (third largest angle in the circle)
   d. 60 pounds – D (smallest angle in the circle)
   e. 270 pounds – B (the largest angle in the circle)

2. $A = 90°$ ($\frac{180}{720} \approx \frac{1}{4}$)

   $B = 135°$ ($\frac{270}{720} \approx \frac{3}{8}$)

   $C = 45°$ ($\frac{90}{720} \approx \frac{1}{8}$)

   $D = 30°$ ($\frac{60}{720} \approx \frac{1}{12}$)

   $E = 60°$ ($\frac{120}{720} \approx \frac{1}{6}$)

TEST 13

DIRECTIONS: The following pictograph shows the growth in production of a shoe company for the period 2008-2014. (Each symbol represents 20,000 pairs of shoes.)

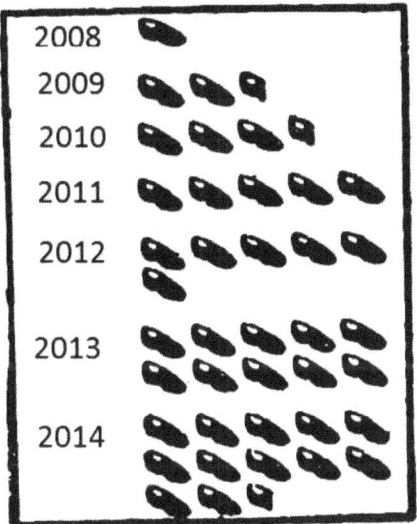

1. How many times as many shoes were produced in 2013 as in 2008? 1.____

2. How many pairs of shoes were produced in 2012? 2.____

3. How many more shoes were produced in 2014 than in 2013? 3.____

2 (#13)

KEY (CORRECT ANSWERS)

1. 10 (10 to 1)

2. 120,000 (6 × 20,000)

3. 50,000 (2½ × 20,000)

INTERPRETING STATISTICAL DATA GRAPHS, CHARTS AND TABLES

EXAMINATION SECTION

TEST 1

DIRECTIONS: Questions 1 through 7 are to be answered SOLELY on the basis of the following graph. *PRINT THE LETTER OF THE CORRECT ANSWER IN THE SPACE AT THE RIGHT.*

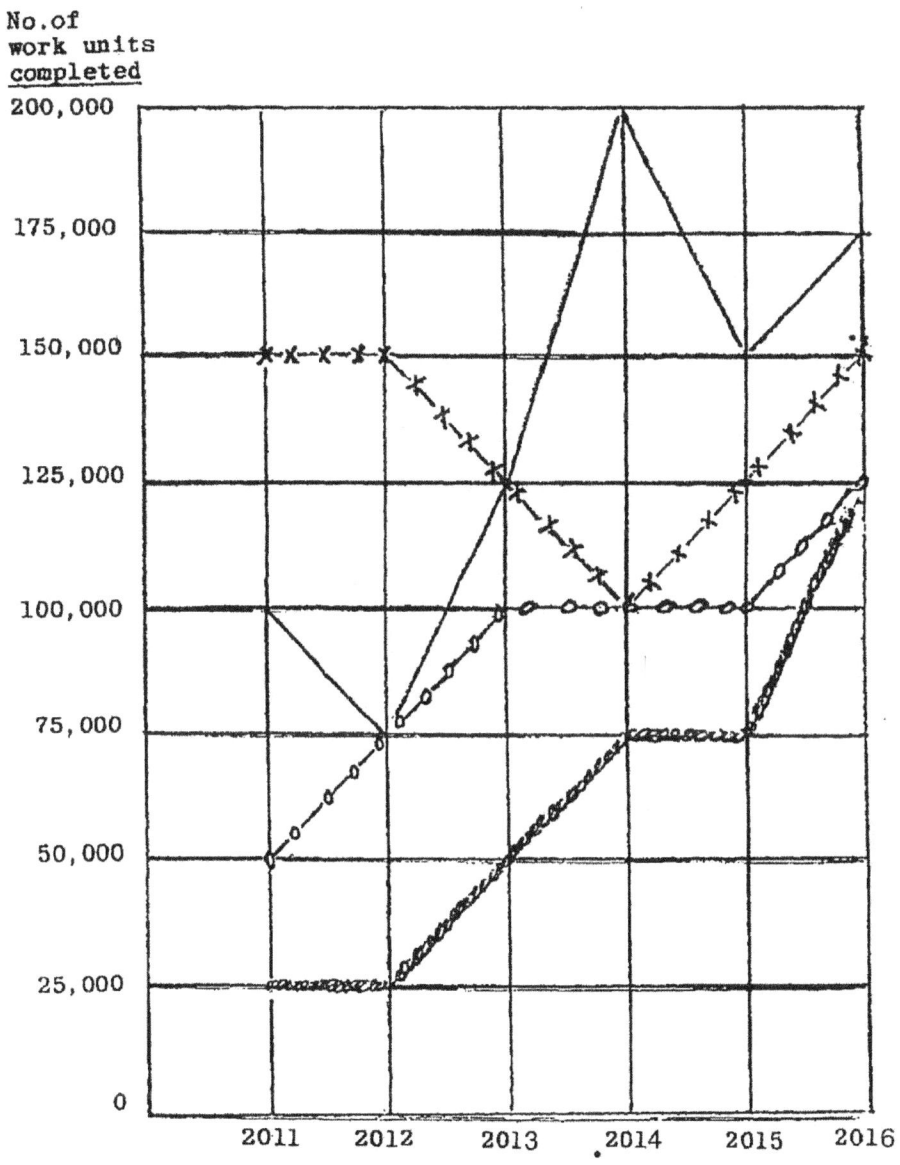

Units of each type of work completed by a public agency from 2011 to 2016.
Letters Written ─────────────
Documents Filed ──X──X──X──X
Applications Processed ──o──o──o──O
Inspections Made ooooooooooooooooooooo

1. The year for which the number of units of one type of work completed was *less* than it was for the previous year while the number of each of the other types of work completed was *more* than it was for the previous year was
    A. 2012   B. 2013   C. 2014   D. 2015

    1.____

2. The number of letters written EXCEEDED the number of applications processed by the *same* amount in _____ of the years.
    A. two   B. three   C. four   D. five

    2.____

3. The year in which the number of each type of work completed was *greater* than in the preceding year was
    A. 2013   B. 2014   C. 2015   D. 2016

    3.____

4. The number of applications processed and the number of documents filed were the SAME in
    A. 2012   B. 2013   C. 2014   D. 2015

    4.____

5. The TOTAL number of units of work completed by the agency
    A. increased in each year after 2011
    B. decreased from the prior year in two of the years after 2011
    C. was the same in two successive years from 2011 to 2016
    D. was less in 2011 than in any of the following years

    5.____

6. For the year in which the number of letters written was twice as high as it was in 2011, the number of documents FILED was _____ it was in 2011.
    A. the same as   B. two-thirds of what
    C. five-sixths of what   D. one and one-half times what

    6.____

7. The variable which was the MOST stable during the period 2011 through 2016 was
    A. Inspections Made   B. Letters Written
    C. Documents Filed   D. Applications Processed

    7.____

KEY (CORRECT ANSWERS)

1. B   5. C
2. B   6. B
3. D   7. B
4. C

TEST 2

DIRECTIONS: Questions 1 through 8 are to be answered SOLELY on the basis of the following graph. *PRINT THE LETTER OF THE CORRECT ANSWER IN THE SPACE AT THE RIGHT.*

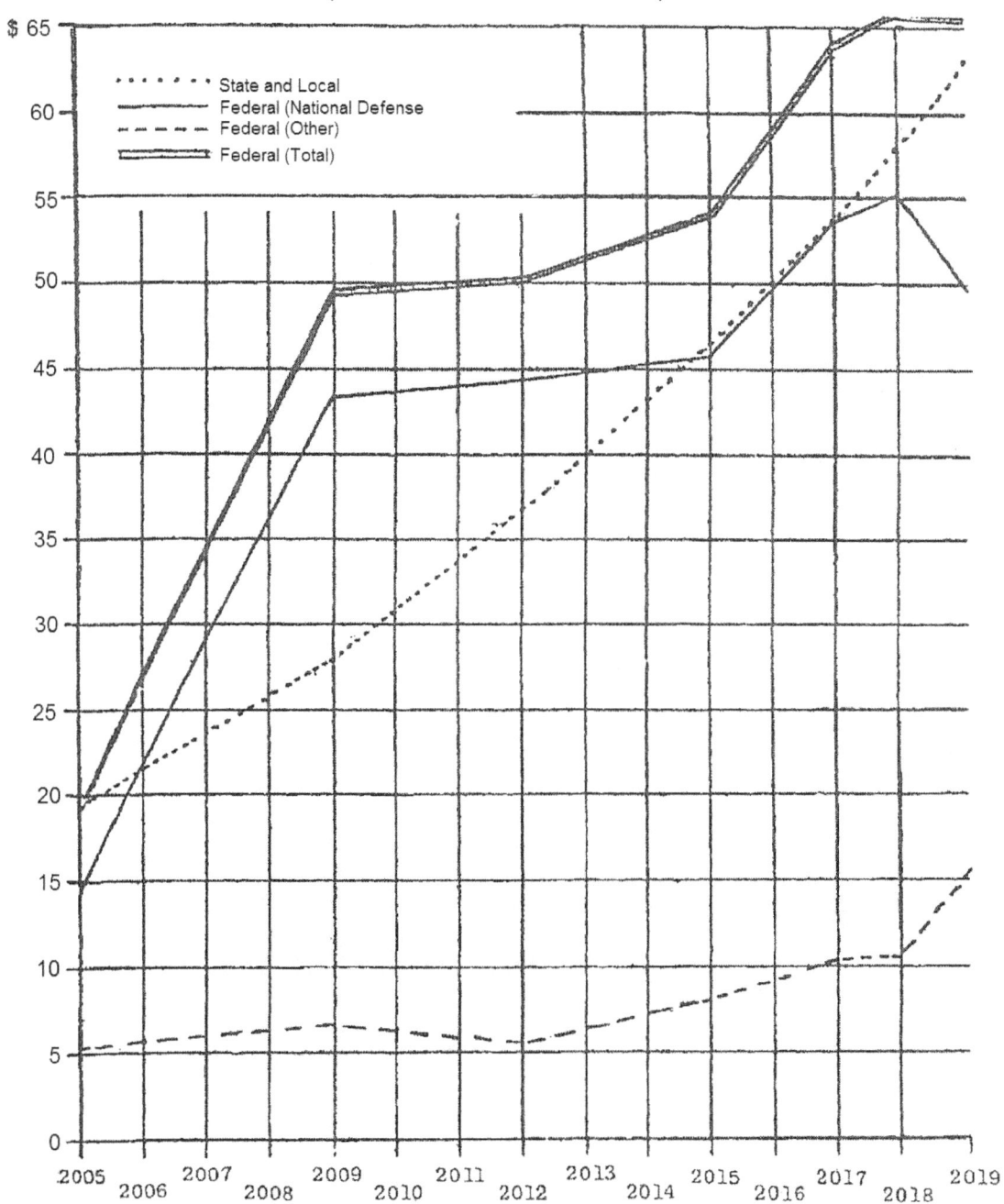

GOVERNMENT PURCHASES OF GOODS AND SERVICES
(IN BILLIONS OF DOLLARS)

2 (#2)

1. Purchases by the Federal government for non-defense purposes, and purchases by State and Local governments comprised the smallest proportion of the total government purchases of goods and services for all purposes in which of the following years?
   A. 2005   B. 2009   C. 2012   D. 2015

   1._____

2. Which one of the following MOST closely approximates the percentage increase in State and Local purchases of goods and services in 2019 as compared to 2005?
   A. 110%   B. 150%   C. 220%   D. 350%

   2._____

3. Total government purchases of goods and services in 2019 was MOST NEARLY _____ billion dollars.
   A. 80   B. 110   C. 128   D. 144

   3._____

4. In 2015, purchases made by State and Local governments
   A. exceeded Federal government total purchases
   B. exceeded purchases made by them in 2009 by more than 50%
   C. increased less than 10% over 2012
   D. were less than 50% of purchases made by them in 2018

   4._____

5. Purchases of goods and services for national defense in 2009 by the Federal government was MOST NEARLY
   A. 15% less than the total spent by Federal, State and Local governments for all purposes in 2005
   B. 50% of the total spent by Federal, State, and Local governments for all purposes in 2012
   C. four times the amount spent in 2005 for National Defense
   D. ten times the amount spent in 2009 by the Federal government for purposes other than National Defense

   5._____

6. In which one of the following years did State and Local purchases of goods and services comprise the GREATEST proportion of the total spent by government jurisdictions?
   A. 2005   B. 2009   C. 2012   D. 2017

   6._____

7. The dollar increase in purchases of goods and services was LEAST for which one of the following?
   A. State and Local governments between 2005 and 2009
   B. State and Local governments between 2012 and 2015
   C. Total Federal government between 2015 and 2017
   D. Federal government other than National Defense between 2015 and 2018

   7._____

8. The rate of increase in Federal purchases of goods and services for National Defense was GREATEST between which of the following periods?
   A. From 2009 to 2012   B. From 2012 and 2015
   C. From 2015 to 2017   D. From 2017 to 2019

   8._____

KEY (CORRECT ANSWERS)

1. B   5. B
2. C   6. A
3. C   7. D
4. B   8. C

TEST 3

DIRECTIONS: Questions 1 through 10 are to be answered SOLELY on the basis of the following table showing the amounts purchased by various purchasing units during 2015. *PRINT THE LETTER OF THE CORRECT ANSWER IN THE SPACE AT THE RIGHT.*

DOLLAR VOLUME PURCHASED BY EACH PURCHASING UNIT DURING EACH QUARTER OF 2015
(Figures Shown Represent Thousands of Dollars)

Purchasing Unit	First Quarter	Second Quarter	Third Quarter	Fourth Quarter
A	578	924	698	312
B	1,426	1,972	1,586	1,704
C	366	494	430	716
D	1,238	1,708	1,884	1,546
E	730	742	818	774
F	948	1,118	1,256	788

1. The TOTAL dollar volume purchased by *all* of the purchasing units during 2015 approximated MOST NEARLY
   A. $2,000,000   B. $4,000,000   C. $20,000,000   D. $40,000,000

2. During which quarter was the GREATEST total dollar amount of purchases made?
   A. First   B. Second   C. Third   D. Fourth

3. Assume that the dollar volume purchased by Unit F during 2015 exceeded the dollar volume purchased by Unit F during 2014 was 50%
   Then, the dollar volume purchased by Unit F during 2014 was
   A. $2,055,000   B. $2,550,000   C. $2,740,000   D. $6,165,000

4. Which one of the following purchasing units showed the SHARPEST decrease in the amount purchased during the *fourth* quarter as compared with the *third* quarter?
   A. A   B. B   C. D   D. E

5. Comparing the dollar volume purchased in the *second* quarter with the dollar volume purchased in the *third* quarter, the decrease in the dollar volume during the third quarter was PRIMARILY due to the decrease in the dollar volume purchased by Units
   A. A and B   B. C and D   C. C and E   D. C and F

6. Of the following, the unit which had the LARGEST number of dollars of increased purchases from any one quarter to the next following quarter was Unit
   A. A   B. B   C. C   D. D

34

3 (#3)

7. Of the following, the unit with the LARGEST dollar volume of purchases during the second half of 2015 was Unit
   A. A   B. B   C. D   D. F

   7.____

8. Which one of the following MOST closely approximates the percentage which Unit B's total 2015 purchases represents of the total 2015 purchases of all units, including Unit B?
   A. 10%   B. 15%   C. 25%   D. 45%

   8.____

9. Assume that research showed that each ten thousand dollars ($10,000) of purchases by Unit D during 2015 required an average of thirteen (13) man-hours of buyers' staff time.
   On that basis, which one of the following MOST closely approximates the number of man-hours of buyers' staff time required by Unit D during 2015?
   A. 1,800   B. 8,000   C. 68,000   D. 78,000

   9.____

10. Assume that research showed that each ten thousand dollars ($10,000) of purchases by Unit C during 2015 required an average of ten (10) man-hours of buyers' staff time. This research also showed that during 2015 the average man-hours of buyers' staff time per ten thousand dollars of purchases required by Unit C exceeded by 25% of the average man-hours of buyers' staff time per ten thousand dollars of purchases required by Unit E.
    On that basis, which one of the following MOST closely approximates the number of buyer's staff man-hours required by Unit E during 2015?
    A. 2,200   B. 2,400   C. 3,000   D. 3,700

    10.____

KEY (CORRECT ANSWERS)

1.	C	6.	B
2.	B	7.	C
3.	C	8.	C
4.	A	9.	B
5.	A	10.	B

TEST 4

DIRECTIONS: Questions 1 through 6 are to be answered SOLELY on the basis of the following table and graph and the accompanying notes. *PRINT THE LETTER OF THE CORRECT ANSWER IN THE SPACE AT THE RIGHT.*

CONSUMER PROTECTION DIVISION-METROPOLITAN CITY
Number and Kinds of Violations (2017-2019)

NATURE OF VIOLATION	2017 District						2018 District						2019 District					
	A	B	C	D	E	Total	A	B	C	D	E	Total	A	B	C	D	E	Total
Scales	27	31	42	16	12	128	18	34	36	15	19	122	20	28	31	12	10	101
Gasoline sales	12	9	17	6	3	47	9	4	19			32	6	5	16	3	6	36
Illegal meat coloring	9	8	13	4		34	10	12	21	9	2	54	8	6	5	2	1	22
Fat content- chopped meat	21	19	40	7	1	88	20	17	31	3	3	74	16	12	18	4	3	53
Checkout counter errors	12	9	10	2		33	12	8	21			41	16	21	9	2	2	50
Fuel oil sales	6	5	4		16	31			2		6	8	5	6	6		18	35
Fraudulent labels	18	29	39	14	14	114	21	36	31	12	18	118	12	25	19	15	25	96
TOTALS	105	110	165	49	46	475	90	111	161	39	48	449	83	103	104	38	65	393

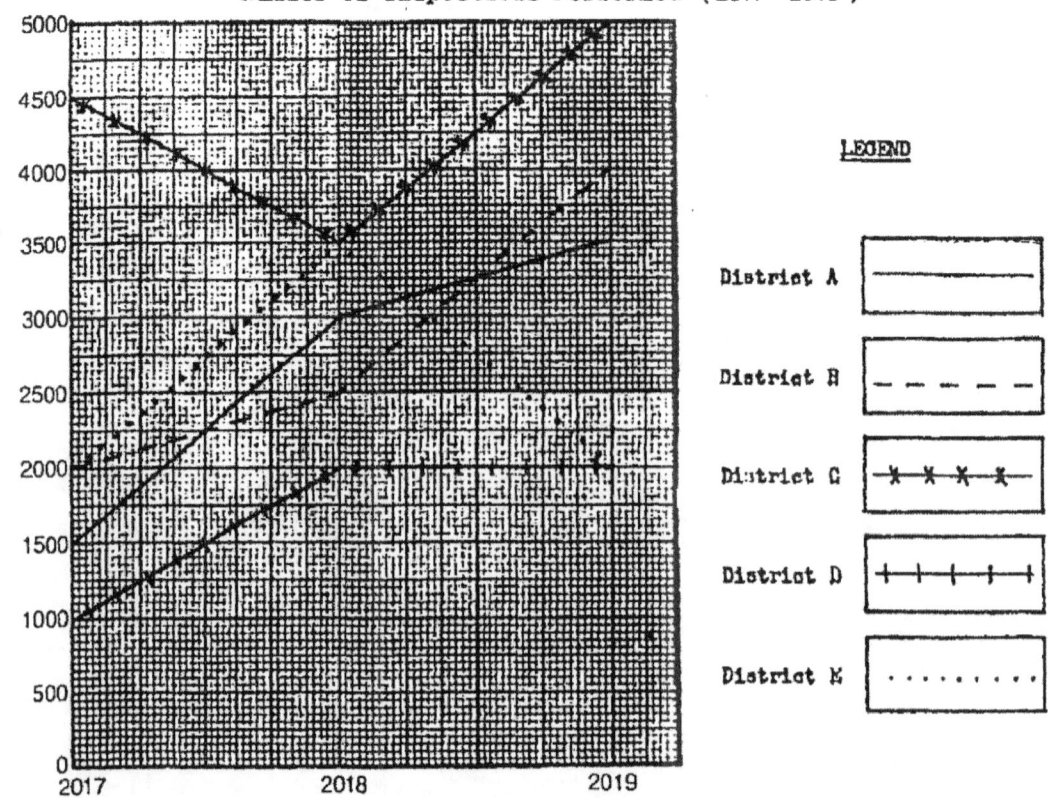

NOTES: The Consumer Protection Division of Metropolitan City is divided into five districts designated A, B, C, D and E.

Number of establishments in each district:
District A – 26,000   District C – 27,000   District E – 12,000
District B – 30,000   District D – 15,000

Number of field inspectors assigned to each district in 2017 and 2018
District A – 20   District C – 25   District E – 11
District B – 24   District D – 21

At the beginning of 2019 there was a general reassignment of field inspectors and the staff of field inspectors was increased. This resulted in assignments of field inspectors as follows:
District A – 20   District C – 32   District E – 16
District B – 26   District D - 16

1. Of the following districts, the one in which the ratio of meat coloring violations to total number of violations in the district was GREATEST in 2018 is District
   A. A B. B C. C D. D

2. In 2018, the number of violations uncovered per field inspector for the entire city was MOST NEARLY
   A. 3.9 B. 4.1 C. 4.4 D. 4.8

3. In 2017, the number of violations per 1,000 establishments in District C was MOST NEARLY
   A. 3.9 B. 6.1 C. 10.4 D. 16.5

4. The number of inspections performed by the Consumer Protection Division in 2018 was MOST NEARLY
   A. 449 B. 12,000 C. 13,500 D. 14,500

5. In 2017, the number of violations uncovered per 100 inspections for the entire city was MOST NEARLY
   A. 23 B. 3.2 C. 4.3 D. 48.0

6. If it had been decided at the beginning of 2019 to assign inspectors so that the ratio of the number of inspectors in each district to the total number of inspectors would be the same as the ratio of the number of establishments in the district to the total number of establishments in the city, the number of inspectors assigned to District A would have been
   A. 24 B. 25 C. 26 D. 17

KEY (CORRECT ANSWERS)

1. D 4. D
2. C 5. C
3. B 6. C

TEST 5

DIRECTIONS: Questions 1 through 4 are to be answered SOLELY on the basis of the following graph and the accompanying notes. *PRINT THE LETTER OF THE CORRECT ANSWER IN THE SPACE AT THE RIGHT.*

NOTES: The graph shows space allocation in three municipal food markets in a certain city. The five columns for each market represent the total amount of each market's space. The miscellaneous column accounts for all non-rental space allocated to shopping aisles, loading facilities, etc.

Assume that during 2019 there was no tenant turnover and that the amount of space rented and unrented remained constant.
The rental charges in 2019 for all types of business were as follows:
  Jefferson Market: $10.00 per square foot
  Jackson Market: $17.50 per square foot
  Lincoln Market: $15.00 per square foot

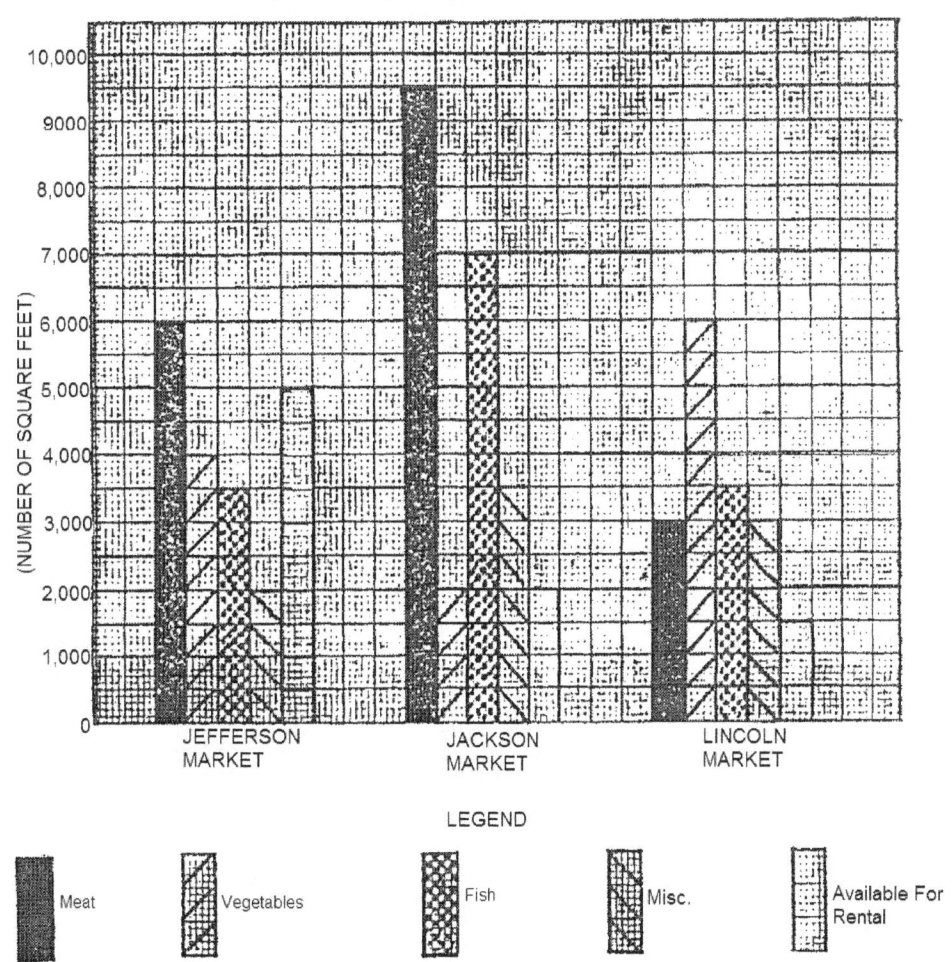

1. The percentage of overall space in the Lincoln Market leased to fish dealers in 2019 is, MOST NEARLY,
   A. 17%   B. 19%   C. 21%   D. 23%

   1.____

2. The total amount of space in all three municipal food markets devoted to the meat business EXCEEDED the amount of space in these markets devoted to the fish business by ____ square feet.
   A. 2,500   B. 4,500   C. 14,000   D. 18,500

   2.____

3. If all of the space in the Lincoln Market available for rental in 2019 had been rented, the income received from this market would have INCREASED by
   A. 6%   B. 12%   C. 18%   D. 24%

   3.____

4. Approximately what percent of the 2019 rental income of the Jackson Market was derived from vegetable dealers?
   A. 8.3%
   B. 9.1%
   C. 10.8%
   D. A percent which cannot be determined from the data given

   4.____

KEY (CORRECT ANSWERS)

1. C
2. B
3. B
4. C

TEST 6

DIRECTIONS: Questions 1 through 5 involve calculation of annual grade averages for college students who have just completed their junior year. These averages are to be based on the following table showing the number of credit hours for each student during the year at each of the grade levels: A, B, C, D, and F. How these letter grades may be translated into numerical grades is indicated in the first column of the table. *PRINT THE LETTER OF THE CORRECT ANSWER IN THE SPACE AT THE RIGHT.*

	Grade Value	Credit Hours – Junior Year					
		King	Lewis	Martin	Norris	Ott	Perry
A =	95	12	12	9	15	6	3
B =	85	9	12	9	12	18	6
C =	75	6	6	9	3	3	21
D =	65	3	3	3	3	-	-
F =	0	-	-	33	-	-	-

NOTES: Calculating a grade average for an individual student is a 4-step process:
I. Multiply each grade value by the number of credit hours for which the student received that grade.
II. Add these multiplication products for each student.
III. Add the student's total credit hours.
IV. Divide the multiplication product total by the total number of credit hours.
V. Round the result, if there is a decimal place, to the nearest whole number. A number ending in .5 would be rounded to the next higher number.

EXAMPLE: Using student King's grades as an example, his grade average can be calculated by going through the following four steps:

I. 95 × 12 = 1140   III. 12
    85 × 9 = 765   9
    75 × 6 = 450   6
    65 × 3 = 195   3
    0 × 0   = 0   0
II. TOTAL   = 2550   30 TOTAL credit hours
                          IV. Divide 2550 by 30: 2550/30 = 85

King's grade average is 85.
Now answer Questions 1 through 5 on the basis of the information given above.

1. The grade average of Lewis is
   A. 83   B. 84   C. 85   D. 86

   1._____

2. The grade average of Martin is
   A. 72   B. 73   C. 74   D. 75

   2._____

3. The grade average of Norris is
   A. 85   B. 86   C. 87   D. 88

   3._____

4. Student Ott must attain a grade average of 90 in each of his years in college to be accepted into the graduate school of his choice.
If, in summer school during his junior year, he takes two 3-credit courses and receives a grade of 95 in each one, his grade average for his junior year will then be MOST NEARLY
   A. 87　　　　B. 88　　　　C. 89　　　　D. 90

5. If Perry takes an additional 3-credit course during the year and receives a grade of 95, his grade average will be increased to APPROXIMATELY
   A. 79　　　　B. 80　　　　C. 89　　　　D. 82

KEY (CORRECT ANSWERS)

1. C
2. D
3. C
4. B
5. B

TEST 7

DIRECTIONS: Questions 1 through 5 are to be answered SOLELY on the basis of the chart below which relates to the increase in taxes. *PRINT THE LETTER OF THE CORRECT ANSWER IN THE SPACE AT THE RIGHT.*

INCREASE IN STATE AND LOCAL TAXES PER PERSON							
	2017	2019	Percent Increase		2017	2019	Percent Increase
Delaware	$138	$372	170	Iowa	$180	$389	116
Maryland	162	411	156	Tennessee	118	252	114
New York	227	576	153	Arkansas	103	221	114
Nebraska	144	362	151	Wyoming	193	414	114
Kentucky	111	278	150	New Mexico	151	324	114
Rhode Island	153	379	148	Idaho	156	328	110
Virginia	128	314	145	Pennsylvania	162	340	109
Arizona	163	387	135	South Dakota	169	353	108
Indiana	141	334	137	Illinois	179	373	108
New Jersey	173	406	135	South Carolina	108	225	108
Wisconsin	187	439	135	Maine	149	308	106
California	232	540	133	Ohio	149	306	105
Michigan	184	428	132	Colorado	189	386	104
Missouri	132	301	128	Nevada	232	466	101
North Carolina	115	259	125	Connecticut	196	392	100
Vermont	173	384	123	Kansas	173	346	100
Minnesota	183	406	122	Texas	139	276	99
West Virginia	119	263	120	Utah	166	327	98
Massachusetts	206	453	119	New Hampshire	152	299	97
Alabama	103	224	118	North Dakota	176	338	92
Washington	189	410	117	Oregon	204	387	90
Florida	153	330	116	Oklahoma	152	287	89
Georgia	125	270	116	Louisiana	160	298	86
Mississippi	112	242	116	Montana	189	351	86

1. The dollar increase per person in taxes between 2017-2019 was GREATEST in which state?
    A. New York
    B. California
    C. Wisconsin
    D. New Jersey
    E. Delaware

1._____

2. The state whose people paid the LOWEST amount per person in taxes in 2019 was
    A. Montana
    B. Mississippi
    C. Alabama
    D. Arkansas
    E. South Carolina

2._____

3. Which of the following states DOUBLED its taxes from 2017 to 2019?
    A. Kentucky
    B. North Carolina
    C. Kansas
    D. Texas
    E. None of the above

3._____

2 (#7)

4. Which state had the SMALLEST increase in taxes from 2017 to 2019?   4._____
   A. Montana   B. Alabama   C. Arkansas
   D. Mississippi   E. South Carolina

5. In which of the following states was the per capita tax the GREATEST in 2017?   5._____
   A. Massachusetts   B. New York   C. Nevada
   D. Delaware   E. Oregon

KEY (CORRECT ANSWERS)

1. A
2. D
3. C
4. E
5. C

TEST 8

DIRECTIONS: Questions 1 through 6 are to be answered SOLELY on the basis of the chart below which relates to the Distribution of Minority Groups by Pay Category. *PRINT THE LETTER OF THE CORRECT ANSWER IN THE SPACE AT THE RIGHT.*

TABLE 1- DISTRIBUTION OF ALL MINORITY GROUPS COMBINED, BY PAY CATEGORY AS OF NOVEMBER 30, 2019 AND MAY 31, 2020

Pay System	November 2019		May 2020		Percent Change
	Number	Percent	Number	Percent	
All Pay Systems	500,508	100.0	501,871	100.0	0.3
General Schedule and Similar	181,725	36.3	186,170	37.1	2.4
Wage Systems	155,744	31.1	151,919	30.3	-2.5
Postal Field Service	158,945	31.8	159,211	31.7	0.2
All Other	4,094	0.8	4,571	0.9	11.7

1. From the table, what was the TOTAL of government workers in *all pay* systems in November 2019?
   A. 155,744
   B. 181,725
   C. 186,170
   D. 500,508
   E. None of the above

   1.____

2. What was the percentage difference between Wage Systems and All Pay Systems in November 2019 and Postal Field Service and All Pay Systems in May 2020?
   A. .2%   B. .6%   C. 1.1%   D. 1.7%   E. 2.5%

   2.____

3. How many more minority group members were employed by the Postal Field Service in May 2020 than in November 2019?
   A. .2%   B. 256   C. 266   D. 1,246   E. 1,266

   3.____

4. In which of the pay systems did the percentage of minority workers decline?
   A. General Schedule and Similar
   B. Wage Systems
   C. Postal Field Service
   D. All Other
   E. None of the above

   4.____

5. In which system was the percentage gain of minority members from 2019 to 2020 the GREATEST?
   A. General Schedule and Similar
   B. Wage Systems
   C. Postal Field Service
   D. All Other Systems
   E. One cannot tell from the information given

   5.____

6. Which system reflects the GREATEST percentage increase from 2019 to 2020 to the total minority work force?
   A. General Schedule and Similar
   B. Wage Systems
   C. Postal Field Service
   D. All Other
   E. One cannot tell from the information given

6.____

KEY (CORRECT ANSWERS)

1. E   4. B
2. B   5. D
3. C   6. A

INTERPRETING STATISTICAL DATA GRAPHS, CHARTS AND TABLES

EXAMINATION SECTION

TEST 1

DIRECTIONS: Each question or incomplete statement is followed by several suggested answers or completions. Select the one that BEST answers the question or completes the statement. *PRINT THE LETTER OF THE CORRECT ANSWER IN THE SPACE AT THE RIGHT.*

Questions 1-10.

DIRECTIONS: Questions 1 through 10 are to be answered SOLELY on the basis of the following table showing the amounts purchased by various purchasing units during 2020.

DOLLAR VOLUME PURCHASED BY EACH PURCHASING UNIT DURING EACH QUARTER OF 2020
(FIGURES SHOWN REPRESENT THOUSANDS OF DOLLARS)

Purchasing Unit	First Quarter	Second Quarter	Third Quarter	Fourth Quarter
A	578	924	698	312
B	1,426	1,972	1,586	1,704
C	366	494	430	716
D	1,238	1,708	1,884	1,546
E	730	742	818	774
F	948	1,118	1,256	788

1. The total dollar volume purchased by all of the purchasing units during 2020 approximated MOST NEARLY
   A. $2,000,000   B. $4,000,000   C. $20,000,000   D. $40,000,000

2. During which quarter was the GREATEST total dollar amount of purchases made?
   A. First   B. Second   C. Third   D. Fourth

3. Assume that the dollar volume purchased by Unit F during 2020 exceeded the dollar volume purchased by Unit F during 2019 by 50%.
   Then, the dollar volume purchased by Unit F during 2019 was
   A. $2,055,000   B. $2,550,000   C. $2,740,000   D. $6,165,000

4. Which one of the following purchasing units showed the sharpest DECREASE in the amount purchased during the fourth quarter as compared with the third quarter?
   A. A   B. B   C. D   D. E

47

5. Comparing the dollar volume purchased in the second quarter with the dollar volume purchased in the third quarter, the decrease in the dollar volume during the third quarter was PRIMARILY due to the decrease in the dollar volume purchased by Units
   A. A and B   B. C and D   C. C and E   D. C and F

6. Of the following, the unit which had the LARGEST number of dollars of increased purchases from any one quarter to the next following quarter was Unit
   A. A   B. B   C. C   D. D

7. Of the following, the unit with the LARGEST dollar volume of purchases during the second half of 2020 was Unit
   A. A   B. B   C. D   D. F

8. Which one of the following MOST closely approximates the percentage which Unit B's total 2020 purchases represents the total 2020 purchases of all units, including Unit B?
   A. 10%   B. 15%   C. 25%   D. 45%

9. Assume that research showed that each ten thousand dollars ($10,000) of purchases by Unit D during 2020 required an average of thirteen (13) man-hours of buyers' staff time.
   On that basis, which one of the following MOST closely approximates the number of man-hours of buyers' staff time required by Unit D during 2020?
   _____ man-hours.
   A. 1,800   B. 8,000   C. 68,000   D. 78,000

10. Assume that research showed that each ten thousand dollars ($10,000) of purchases by Unit C during 020 required an average of ten (10) man-hours of buyers' staff time. This research also showed that during 2020 the average man-hours of buyers' staff time per ten thousand dollars of purchases required by Unit C exceeded by 25% the average man-hours of buyers' staff time per ten thousand dollars of purchases required by Unit E.
    On that basis, which one of the following MOST closely approximates the number of buyers' staff man-hours required by Unit E during 2020?
    _____ man-hours.
    A. 2,200   B. 2,400   C. 3,000   D. 3,700

KEY (CORRECT ANSWERS)

1. C
2. B
3. C
4. A
5. A
6. B
7. C
8. C
9. B
10. B

TEST 2

Questions 1-6.

DIRECTIONS: Questions 1 through 6 are to be answers SOLELY on the basis of the information contained in the five charts below. *PRINT THE LETTER OF THE CORRECT ANSWER IN THE SPACE AT THE RIGHT.*

NUMBER OF UNITS OF WORK PRODUCED IN THE BUREAU PER YEAR

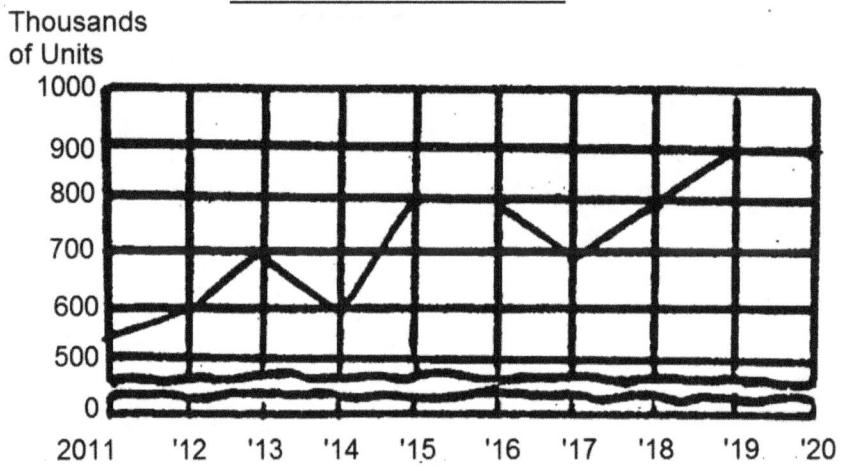

INCREASE IN THE NUMBER OF UNITS OF WORK PRODUCED IN 2020 OVER THE NUMBER PRODUCED IN 2011, BY BOROUGH

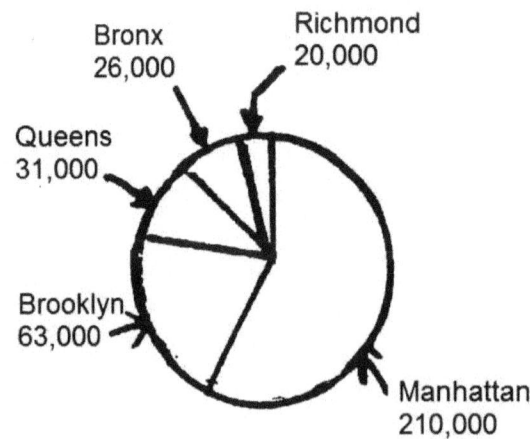

Bronx 26,000
Richmond 20,000
Queens 31,000
Brooklyn 63,000
Manhattan 210,000

NUMBER OF MALE AND FEMALE EMPLOYEES PRODUCING THE UNITS OF WORK IN THE BUREAU PER YEAR

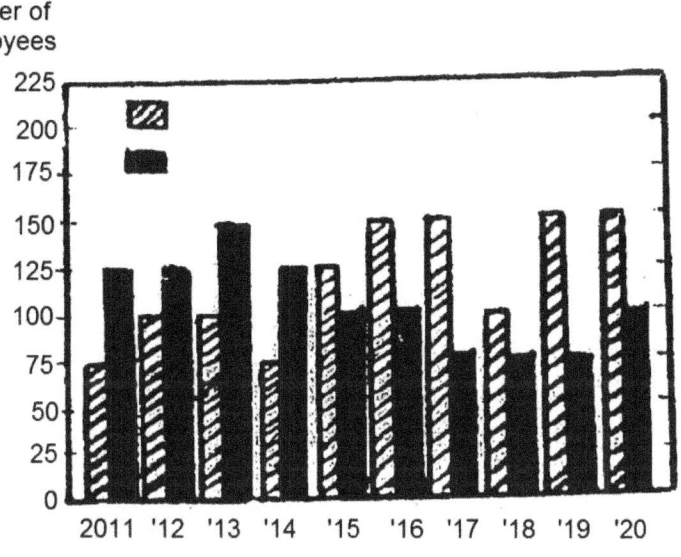

DISTRIBUTION OF THE AGES BY PERCENT OF EMPLOYEES ASSIGNED TO PRODUCE THE UNITS OF WORK IN THE YEARS 2011 AND 2020

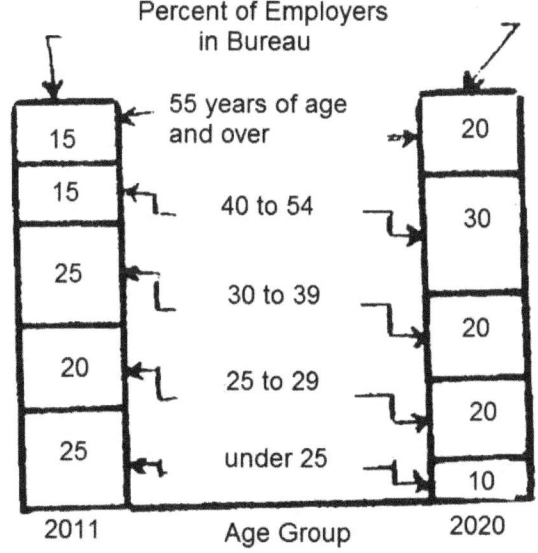

TOTAL SALARIES PAID PER YEAR TO EMPLOYEES ASSIGNED TO PRODUCE THE UNITS OF WORK IN THE BUREAU

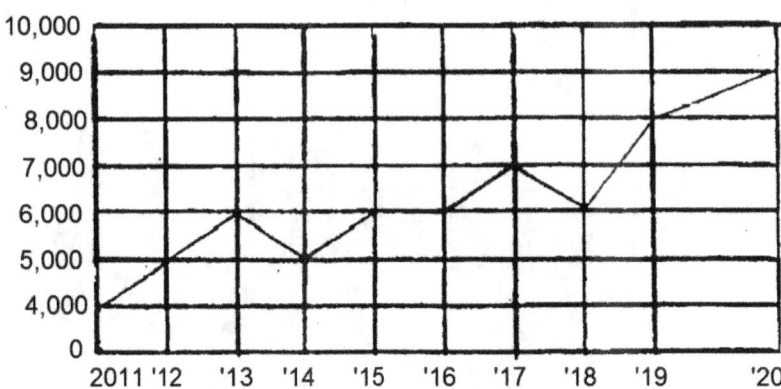

1. The information contained in the charts is sufficient to determine the
    A. amount of money paid in salaries to employees working in Richmond in 2020
    B. difference between the average annual salary of employees in the Bureau in 2020 and their average annual salary in 2019
    C. number of female employees in the Bureau between 30 and 39 years of age who were employed in 2011
    D. cost, in salary, for the average male employee in the Bureau to produce 100 units of work in 2016

2. The one of the following which was GREATER in the Bureau in 2016 than it was in 2014 was the
    A. cost, in salaries, of producing a unit of work
    B. units of work produced annually per employee
    C. proportion of female employees to total number of employees
    D. average annual salary per employee

3. If, in 2020, one-half of the employees in the Bureau 55 years of age and over each earned an annual salary of $42,000, then the average annual salary of all the remaining employees in the Bureau was MOST NEARLY
    A. $31,750   B. $34,500   C. $35,300   D. $35,800

4. Assume that, in 2011, the offices in Richmond and the Bronx each produced the same number of units of work. Also assume that, in 2011, the offices in Brooklyn, Manhattan, and Queens each produced twice as many units of work as were produced in either of the other two boroughs.
   Then, the number of units of work produced in Brooklyn in 2010 was MOST NEARLY
    A. 69,000   B. 138,000   C. 201,000   D. 225,000

5. If, in 2008, the average annual salary of the female employees in the Bureau was four-fifths as large as the average annual salary of the male employees, then the average annual salary of the female employees in that year was
   A. $37,500   B. $31,000   C. $30,500   D. $30,000

6. Of the total number of employees in the Bureau who were 30 years of age and over in 2011, _____ must have been _____.
   A. at least 35; females
   B. less than 75; males
   C. no more than 100; females
   D. more than 15; males

KEY (CORRECT ANSWERS)

1. B   4. C
2. B   5. D
3. C   6. A

TEST 3

Questions 1-10.

DIRECTIONS: Questions 1 through 10 are to be answered SOLELY on the basis of the REPORT OF TELEPHONE CALLS table given below. *PRINT THE LETTER OF THE CORRECT ANSWER IN THE SPACE AT THE RIGHT.*

TABLE – REPORT OF TELEPHONE CALLS							
Dept.	No. of Stations	No. of Employees	No. of Incoming Calls		No. of Long Distance Calls		No. of Divisions
			2019	2020	2019	2020	
I	11	40	3421	4292	72	54	5
II	36	220	10392	10191	75	78	18
III	53	250	85243	85084	103	98	8
IV	24	60	9675	10123	82	85	6
V	13	30	5208	5492	54	48	6
VI	25	35	7472	8109	86	90	5
VII	37	195	11412	11299	68	72	11
VIII	36	54	8467	8674	59	68	4
IX	163	306	294321	289968	289	321	13
X	40	83	9588	8266	93	89	5
XI	24	68	7867	7433	86	87	13
XII	50	248	10039	10208	101	95	30
XIII	10	230	7550	6941	28	21	10
XIV	25	103	14281	14392	48	40	5
XV	19	230	8475	9206	38	43	8
XVI	22	45	4684	5584	39	48	10
XVII	41	58	10102	9677	49	52	6
XVIII	82	106	106242	105899	128	132	10
XIX	6	13	2649	2498	35	29	2
XX	16	30	1395	1468	7890	2	

1. The department which had more than 106,000 incoming calls in 2019 but fewer than 250,000 is
   A. II   B. IX   C. XVIII   D. III

   1.____

2. The department which has fewer than 8 divisions and more than 100 but fewer than 300 employees is
   A. VII   B. XIV   C. XV   D. XVIII

   2.____

3. The department which had an increase in 2020 over 2019 in the number of both incoming and long distance calls but had an increase in long distance calls of not more than 3 is
   A. IV   B. VI   C. XVII   D. XVIII

   3.____

2 (#3)

4. The department which had a decrease in the number of incoming calls in 2020 as compared to 2019 and has not less than 6 nor more than 7 divisions is
   A. IV   B. V   C. XVII   D. III

   4._____

5. The department which has more than 7 divisions and more than 200 employees but fewer than 19 stations is
   A. XV   B. III   C. XX   D. XIII

   5._____

6. The department having more than 10 divisions and fewer than 36 stations, which had an increase in long distance calls in 2020 over 2019 is
   A. XI   B. VII   C. XVI   D. XVIII

   6._____

7. The department which in 2020 had at least 7,250 incoming calls and a decrease in long distance calls from 2019, and has more than 50 stations is
   A. IX   B. XII   C. XVIII   D. III

   7._____

8. The department which has fewer than 25 stations, fewer than 100 employees, 10 or more divisions, and showed an increase of at least 9 long distance calls in 2020 over 2019 is
   A. IX   B. XVI   C. XX   D. XIII

   8._____

9. The department which has more than 50 but fewer than 125 employee and had more than 5,000 incoming calls in 2019 but not more than 10,000, and more than 60 long distance calls in 2020 but not more than 85, and has more than 24 stations is
   A. VIII   B. XIV   C. IV   D. XI

   9._____

10. If the number of departments showing an increase in long distance calls in 2020 over 2019 exceeds the number showing a decrease in long distance calls in the same period, select the Roman numeral indicating the department having less than one station for each 10 employees, provided not more than 8 divisions are served by that department.
    If the number of departments showing an increase in long distance calls in 2020 over 2019 does not exceed the number showing a decrease in long distance calls in the same period, select the Roman numeral indicating the department having the SMALLEST number of incoming calls in 2020.
    A. III   B. XIII   C. XV   D. XX

    10._____

KEY (CORRECT ANSWERS)

1. C
2. B
3. A
4. C
5. D
6. A
7. D
8. B
9. A
10. C

TEST 4

Questions 1-7.

DIRECTIONS: Questions 1 through 7 are to be answered SOLELY on the basis of the following chart. *PRINT THE LETTER OF THE CORRECT ANSWER IN THE SPACE AT THE RIGHT.*

EMPLOYABILITY CLASSIFICATION OF PERSONS RECEIVING HOME RELIEF OR VETERANS' ASSISTANCE AT WELFARE CENTER V, JANUARY 1, THIS YEAR				
Employability Classification	Home Relief		Veterans' Assistance	
	Full	Supplementary	Full	Supplementary
Employable	369	207	15	42
Employed	330	83	2	35
Not Available for Employment	550	129	27	93
Awaiting employment conference	24	4	1	3
In rehabilitation	81	18	1	21
Attending school	26	16	3	13
In training	78	24	4	4
Temporary family care duties	32	19	6	7
Permanent family care duties	166	7	8	25
Unverified health condition	77	22	1	3
Temporary health condition	66	19	3	17
Permanently unemployable	47	8	1	37
TOTAL	1296	427	45	207

1. Of the persons on Home Relief who are either employed or employable, the percentage who are employable and are receiving full assistance is MOST NEARLY
   A. 30% B. 35% C. 50% D. 65%

   1.____

2. Assume that it is possible each month to reduce the number of Home Relief clients who are not available for employment and who are receiving full assistance by 10% from the previous month.
   By June 1, this year, the number of such Home Relief clients would be MOST NEARLY
   A. 225 B. 275 C. 325 D. 375

   2.____

3. During the month of January, this year, of the full-assistance clients on Home Relief who were not available for employment because of temporary health conditions, 42% were removed from the relief rolls, and another 26% were reassigned to supplementary Home Relief assistance because of temporary health conditions.
   Taking figures to the nearest whole number, the number of all remaining Home Relief clients, including both full and supplementary assistance at Welfare Center V is MOST NEARLY
   A. 1250 B. 1265 C. 1675 D. 1695

   3.____

2 (#4)

4. The one of the following figures which is MOST likely to require checking for accuracy or investigating for significance is the figure for persons
   A. not available for employment who are receiving supplementary Veterans' Assistance
   B. receiving full Home Relief assistance who are employed
   C. receiving supplementary Home Relief assistance who are not available for employment because they are in rehabilitation
   D. receiving supplementary Veterans' Assistance who are permanently unemployable

5. With regard to clients receiving full Veterans' Assistance, the average monthly allotment per client in the various categories is as follows: Employable $168.06; Employed $194.92; Not Available for Employment $130.74; and Permanently Unemployable $112.56.
   The average monthly allotment for all clients receiving full Veterans' Assistance at Welfare Center V is MOST NEARLY
   A. $140.06   B. $145.64   C. $151.58   D. $162.26

6. If all the Employable Home Relief clients on full assistance were to find employment so that 2/3 of them would no longer need any assistance and the rest would need only supplementary assistance, then the ratio of all Home Relief clients on full assistance to all Home Relief clients on supplementary assistance would be MOST NEARLY
   A. 2:1   B. 3:1   C. 3:2   D. 5:3

7. Assume that, for the category of Veterans' Assistance, the Federal government were to pay 2/3 of the first $60 of assistance given to each client, and 1/2 of the balance, on the basis of the average amount of assistance given to all veterans at a welfare center. Assume further that the average supplementary assistance given is $72, and the average full assistance is $140 at Welfare Center V.
   Under this plan, the amount of Veterans' Assistance given by Welfare Center V for which they would be reimbursed by the Federal government will be MOST NEARLY
   A. $8,000   B. $11,000   C. $13,000   D. $17,000

KEY (CORRECT ANSWERS)

1. B
2. C
3. D
4. B
5. B
6. D
7. C

TEST 5

Questions 1-10.

DIRECTIONS: Questions 1 through 10 are to be answered SOLELY on the basis of the Personnel Record of Division X shown below. *PRINT THE LETTER OF THE CORRECT ANSWER IN THE SPACE AT THE RIGHT.*

				No. of Days Absent		
Employee	Bureau in Which Employed	Title	Annual Salary	On Vacation	On Sick Leave	No. of Times Late
Abbott	Mail	Clerk	$31,200	18	0	1
Barnes	Mail	Clerk	$25,200	25	3	7
Davis	Mail	Typist	$24,000	21	9	2
Adams	Payroll	Accountant	$42,500	10	0	2
Bell	Payroll	Bookkeeper	$31,200	23	2	5
Duke	Payroll	Clerk	$27,600	24	4	3
Gross	Payroll	Clerk	$21,600	12	5	7
Lane	Payroll	Stenographer	$26,400	19	16	20
Reed	Payroll	Typist	$22,800	15	11	11
Arnold	Record	Clerk	$32,400	6	15	9
Cane	Record	Clerk	$24,500	14	3	4
Fay	Record	Clerk	$21,100	20	0	4
Hale	Record	Typist	$25,200	18	2	7
Baker	Supply	Clerk	$30,000	20	3	2
Clark	Supply	Clerk	$27,600	25	6	5
Ford	Supply	Typist	$22,800	25	4	22

(Division X Personnel Record – Current Year)

1. The percentage of the total number of employees who are clerks is MOST NEARLY
   A. 25%   B. 33%   C. 38%   D. 56%

2. Of the following employees, the one who receives a monthly salary of $2,100 is
   A. Barnes   B. Gross   C. Reed   D. Clark

3. The difference between the annual salary of the highest paid clerk and that of the lowest paid clerk is
   A. $6,000   B. $8,400   C. $11,300   D. $20,900

4. The number of employees receiving more than $25,000 a year but less than $40,000 a year is
   A. 6   B. 9   C. 12   D. 15

5. The TOTAL annual salary of the employees of the Mail Bureau is _____ the total annual salary of the employees of the _____.
   A. one-half of; Payroll Bureau
   B. less than; Record Bureau by $21,600
   C. equal to; Supply Bureau
   D. less than; Payroll Bureau by $71,600

2 (#5)

6. The average annual salary of the employees who are not clerks is MOST NEARLY
   A. $23,700   B. $25,450   C. $26,800   D. $27,850

   6.____

7. If all the employees were given a 10% increase in pay, the annual salary of Lane would then be
   A. *greater* than that of Barnes by $1,320
   B. *less* than that of Bell by $4,280
   C. *equal* to that of Clark
   D. *greater* than that of Ford by $3,600

   7.____

8. Of the clerks who earned less than $30,000 a year, the one who was late the FEWEST number of times was late _____ time(s).
   A. 1   B. 2   C. 3   D. 4

   8.____

9. The bureau in which the employees were late the FEWEST number of times on an average age is the _____ Bureau.
   A. Mail   B. Payroll   C. Record   D. Supply

   9.____

10. The MOST accurate of the following statements is that:
    A. Reed was late more often than any other typist
    B. Bell took more time off for vacation than any other employee earning $30,000 or more annually
    C. of the typist, Ford was the one who was absent the fewest number of times
    D. three clerks took no time off because of sickness

    10.____

KEY (CORRECT ANSWERS)

1.	D	6.	D
2.	A	7.	A
3.	C	8.	C
4.	B	9.	A
5.	C	10.	B

TEST 6

Questions 1-8.

DIRECTIONS: Questions 1 through 8 are to be answered SOLELY on the basis of the information contained in the chart and table shown below which relate to Bureau X in a certain public agency. The chart shows the percentage of the bureau's annual expenditures spent on equipment, supplies, and salaries for each of the years 2016-2020. The table shows the bureau's annual expenditures for each of the years 2016-2020. *PRINT THE LETTER OF THE CORRECT ANSWER IN THE SPACE AT THE RIGHT.*

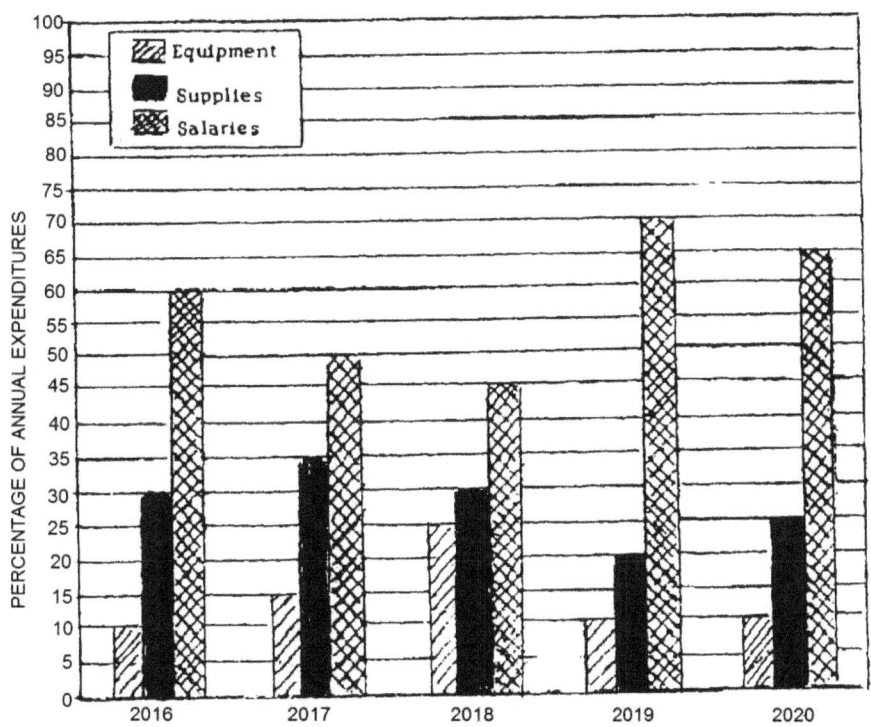

The bureau's annual expenditures for the years 2016-2020 are shown in the following table:

YEAR	EXPENDITURES
2016	$8,000,000
2017	$12,000,000
2018	$15,000,000
2019	$10,000,000
2020	$12,000,000

Equipment, supplies, and salaries were the only three categories for which the bureau spent money.

Candidates may find it useful to arrange their computations on their scratch paper in an orderly manner since the correct computations for one question may also be helpful in answering another question.

1. The information contained in the chart and table is sufficient to determine the
   A. average annual salary of an employee in the bureau in 2017
   B. decrease in the amount of money spent on supplies in the bureau in 2016 from the amount spent in the preceding year
   C. changes between 2018 and 2019 in the prices of supplies bought by the bureau
   D. increase in the amount of money spent on salaries in the bureau in 2020 over the amount spent in the preceding year

1.____

2. If the percentage of expenditures for salaries in one year is added to the percentage of expenditures for equipment in that year, a total of two percentages for that year is obtained.
   The two years for which this total is the SAME are
   A. 2016 and 2018
   B. 2017 and 2019
   C. 2016 and 2019
   D. 2017 and 2020

2.____

3. Of the following, the year in which the bureau spent the GREATEST amount of money on supplies was
   A. 2020   B. 2018   C. 2017   D. 2016

3.____

4. Of the following years, the one in which there was the GREATEST increase over the preceding year in the amount of money spent on salaries is
   A. 2019   B. 2020   C. 2017   D. 2018

4.____

5. Of the bureau's expenditures for equipment in 2020, one-third was used for the purchase of mailroom equipment and the remainder was spent on miscellaneous office equipment.
   How much did the bureau spend on miscellaneous office equipment in 2020?
   A. $4,000,000   B. $400,000   C. $8,000,000   D. $800,000

5.____

6. If there were 120 employees in the bureau in 2019, then the average annual salary paid to the employees in that year was MOST NEARLY
   A. $43,450   B. $49,600   C. $58,350   D. $80,800

6.____

7. In 2018, the bureau had 125 employees.
   If 20 of the employees earned an average annual salary of $80,000, then the average salary of the other 105 employees was MOST NEARLY
   A. $49,000   B. $64,000   C. $41,000   D. $54,000

7.____

8. Assume that the bureau estimated that the amount of money it would spend on supplies in 2021 would be the same as the amount it spent on that category in 2020. Similarly, the bureau estimated that the amount of money it would spend on equipment in 2021 would be the same as the amount it spent on that category in 2020. However, the bureau estimated that in 2021 the amount it would spent on salaries would be 10 percent higher than the amount it spent on that category in 2020.
The percentage of its annual expenditures that the bureau estimated it would spend on supplies in 2021 is MOST NEARLY
   A. 27.5%   B. 23.5%   C. 22.5%   D. 25%

8._____

KEY (CORRECT ANSWERS)

1. D   5. D
2. A   5. C
3. B   7. A
4. C   8. B

TEST 7

Questions 1-5.

DIRECTIONS: Column I lists five kinds of statistical data which are to be transformed into a chart or a graph for incorporation into the department annual report. Column II lists nine different kinds of graphs or charts. For each type of information listed in Column I, select the chart or graph from Column II by means of which it should be demonstrated. *PRINT THE LETTER OF THE CORRECT ANSWER IN THE SPACE AT THE RIGHT.*

Column I

1. The relationship between employees' occupational classification and their salaries, for all employees by occupational classification, showing minimum, maximum, and average salary in each group.

2. A comparison of the number of employees in the department, the departmental budget, the number of employees in the operating divisions and the operating division budget for each year over a ten-year period.

3. The amount of money spent for each of department's 10 most important functions during the past year

4. The percentage of the department's budget spent for each of the department's activities for each year over a ten-year period.

5. The number of each kind of employee employed in the department over a period of twenty years and the total number of employees in the department for each of these periods.

Column II

A.

B.

C.

D.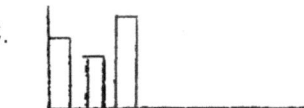

E.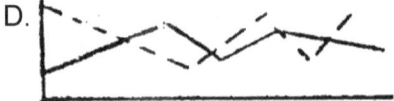

F.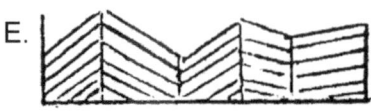

G.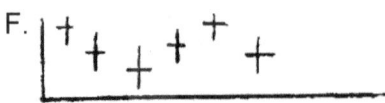

H.

1.____

2.____

3.____

4.____

5.____

KEY (CORRECT ANSWERS)

1. F
2. D
3. C
4. H
5. G

INTERPRETING STATISTICAL DATA
GRAPHS, CHARTS AND TABLES
TEST 1

DIRECTIONS: Each question or incomplete statement is followed by several suggested answers or completions. Select the one that BEST answers the question or completes the statement. *PRINT THE LETTER OF THE CORRECT ANSWER IN THE SPACE AT THE RIGHT.*

Questions 1-5.

DIRECTIONS: Questions 1 through 5 are to be answered according to the information given in the following chart.

COLLECTION DIVISION
PARKING METER FIELD
OPERATION REPORT

Date: Jan. 4

Location	Time Arrived	Time Departed	Elapsed Time	
			Travel	Collection
			Hr. Min.	Hr. Min.
Office		9:15		
2407	10:00	10:35	45	35
3502	10:45	11:15	10	30
2574	11:20	12:50	5	1 30
Lunch	1:05	2:05	15	
3379	2:05	2:55		50
2810	3:05	3:30	10	25
3208	3:35	4:00	5	25
Office	4:45		45	
		Total_____		

Remarks: _____

Mileage	Start	174	Vehicle No.	12		
	Close	209	Total Crew	3		
Daily Total		35				
			Parking Meter Areas Assigned:	2407,	3502,	
				2574,	3379,	
				2810,	3208	
			James Roe			
			Driver			

67

1. According to the information in the report and assuming equal traffic conditions, which of the following statements about the distances between locations is TRUE?

    A. If the crew car was always driven at an average speed of 25 miles an hour, the crew never travelled less than 2 miles to get from one location to another.
    B. The last location the crew worked at was farther from the office than the first location they worked at.
    C. The place where the crew ate lunch was right near the last place they worked at before lunch.
    D. Travelling from one assigned parking meter area to the next, the crew never travelled as far as when they went from the first to the second location they worked at.

2. Which of the following items of information can be obtained from the report?

    A. Average time spent collecting at each location
    B. The license of the vehicle
    C. When the crew got to the office in the morning
    D. When the crew left the office in the afternoon

3. Suppose that, on the average, the same amount of time was spent by a parking meter collector in collecting from any meter.
   Therefore, according to the report, the parking meter area that had approximately 1/3 as many meters as Area 2574 is

    A. 2407   B. 3502   C. 3379   D. 2810

4. Information which CANNOT be obtained from this report alone is the

    A. distance travelled
    B. total time spent collecting
    C. number of meters collected from
    D. total time spent travelling

5. Judging from the information in the report, it is MOST probable that

    A. members of the crew took turns driving
    B. nothing unusual happened to this crew that day
    C. the crew did not take their full time for lunch
    D. the crew was made up of a driver and a collector

KEY (CORRECT ANSWERS)

1. A
2. A
3. B
4. C
5. B

TEST 2

Questions 1-8.

DIRECTIONS: Questions 1 through 8 are to be answered ONLY on the basis of the information contained in the following table. Each question consists of a statement. You are to indicate whether the statement is TRUE (T) or FALSE (F). *PRINT THE LETTER OF THE CORRECT ANSWER IN THE SPACE AT THE RIGHT.*

SUMMONS RECORD

District	No. of Summonses Issued 2016	2017	No. Dismissed 2016	2017
Oakdale	3,250	3,147	650	631
Marlboro	2,410	2,320	670	718
Eastchester	3,502	3,710	800	825
Kensington	10,423	10,218	2,317	2,343
Glenridge	5,100	5,250	1,200	1,213
Seaside	4,864	4,739	1,469	1,375
Darwin	3,479	3,661	815	826
Ulster	4,100	3,789	1,025	1,000
Totals	37,128	?	8,946	?

1. In most of the districts, the number of summonses dismissed was greater in 2017 than in 2016.   1.____

2. In most of the districts, the number of summonses issued was smaller in 2016 than in 2017.   2.____

3. The district which had the smallest number of summonses issued in 2016 also had the smallest number of summonses dismissed in 2016.   3.____

4. The two districts which issued the largest number of summonses in 2017 also dismissed the largest number of summonses in 2017.   4.____

5. The district that was second in the number of summonses issued both years was also second in the number of summonses dismissed both years.   5.____

6. The total number of summonses dismissed in 2017 is 15 less than the total number dismissed in 2016.   6.____

7. In 2017 there was a greater difference between the two districts with the smallest and largest number of summonses dismissed than in 2016.   7.____

8. The total number of summonses issued in 2016 is 294 greater than the total number of summonses issued in 2017.   8.____

KEY (CORRECT ANSWERS)

1. T
2. F
3. F
4. F
5. F
6. T
7. T
8. T

TEST 3

Questions 1-7.

DIRECTIONS: Questions 1 through 7 are to be answered ONLY on the basis of the information given in the table below.

RECEIVING AND SHIPPING RECORD

Hospital	Item	Received Date	Amount	Shipped Date	Amount
Hughes	Bibs, Child	2/2	30	2/11	24
	Bibs, Adult	2/5	25	2/11	19
	Gowns	2/17	17	3/3	17
	Towels, Hand	2/18	16	2/25	16
	Bathrobes, Adult	2/20	20	3/3	18
	Bathrobes, Child	2/23	15	3/17	15
	Bathrobes, Adult	2/23	12	3/5	10
Lehman	Towels, Bath	2/5	15	2/25	13
	Sheets, Crib	2/10	8	2/18	6
	Sheets, Bassinet	2/10	15	2/20	12
	Sheets, Crib	2/10	23	2/19	23
	Spreads, Large	2/23	26	3/4	25
	Spreads, Crib	2/23	10	3/5	10
	Towels, Hand	2/25	17	3/5	17
Smith	Sheets, Crib	2/5	15	3/1	12
	Pillowcases	2/10	16	2/18	14
	Sheets, Large	2/10	30	2/18	21
	Sheets, Crib	2/11	20	2/18	18
	Towels, Hand	2/17	25	2/25	14
	Towels, Bath	2/19	18	2/25	15

1. The one item received from Hughes Hospital for laundering on 2/2 is

    A. towels, hand
    B. sheets, large
    C. bibs, child
    D. sheets, crib

2. The TOTAL number of sheets shipped to Smith Hospital on 2/18 is

    A. 29   B. 39   C. 50   D. 51

3. The date on which crib spreads were shipped to Lehman Hospital is

    A. 2/18   B. 2/19   C. 3/4   D. 3/5

4. The TOTAL number of bathrobes received from Hughes Hospital on 2/23 is

    A. 27   B. 32   C. 35   D. 47

5. The TOTAL number of hand towels shipped on 2/25 to all hospitals is

    A. 29   B. 30   C. 42   D. 43

6. The TOTAL number of sheets received from all hospitals on 2/10 is

    A. 46   B. 76   C. 86   D. 106

7. Which one of the following items is listed ONLY for Smith Hospital?

   A. Bibs, child
   B. Spreads, large
   C. Gowns
   D. Pillowcases

KEY (CORRECT ANSWERS)

1. C
2. B
3. D
4. A
5. B
6. B
7. D

TEST 4

Questions 1-6.

DIRECTIONS: Questions 1 through 6 are to be answered ONLY on the basis of the information contained in the chart below, which shows the number of requisitions filled by Storeroom A during each month of 2018.

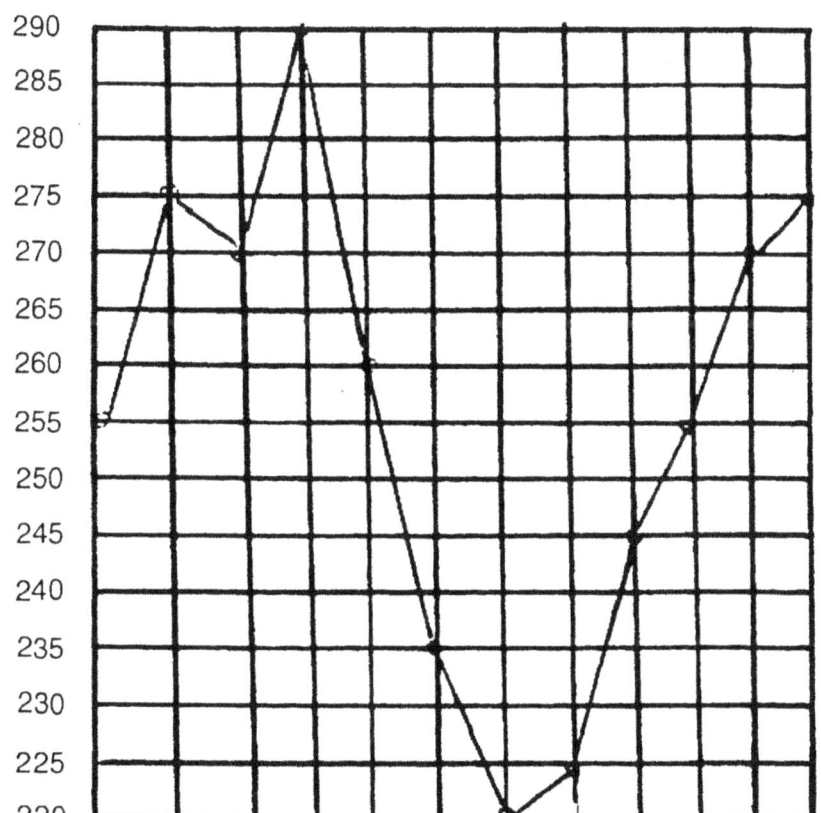

1. According to the above chart, the average number of requisitions handled per month by Storeroom A during the first six months of 2018 is MOST NEARLY

    A. 250 B. 260 C. 270 D. 280

2. It is expected that the number of requisitions Storeroom A will handle in 2019 will be 10 percent more than it handled in 2018.
   The number of requisitions Storeroom A is expected to handle during 2019 is

    A. 2,763 B. 3,070 C. 3,377 D. 3,440

73

3. The month during which the number of requisitions handled showed the GREATEST decrease from the previous month was

    A. April   B. May   C. June   D. July

3.____

4. During May there were 3 clerks assigned to Storeroom A. One man went on vacation for the month of June and was not replaced.
The number of additional orders handled by each man working in June over the number of orders handled per man in May was MOST NEARLY

    A. 20   B. 27   C. 32   D. 36

4.____

5. During June, July, and August, 8 percent of the requisitions handled were rush orders. The number of rush orders handled during these three months is MOST NEARLY

    A. 55   B. 60   C. 65   D. 70

5.____

6. During November, there were three clerks assigned to Storeroom A.
If one handled 95 requisitions and another handled 85 requisitions, the number of requisitions handled by the third clerk was

    A. 70   B. 80   C. 90   D. 100

6.____

KEY (CORRECT ANSWERS)

1. B
2. C
3. B
4. C
5. A
6. C

TEST 5

Questions 1-3.

DIRECTIONS: Questions 1 through 3 are to be answered ONLY on the basis of the information given below.

At midnight of each day, readings are made of gas consumption meters. Readings for 8 days are as follows:

Sunday	6873	cu. ft.	Thursday	3256	cu. ft.
Monday	8147	cu. ft.	Friday	4962	cu. ft.
Tuesday	0065	cu. ft.	Saturday	6823	cu. ft.
Wednesday	1480	cu. ft.	Sunday	7179	cu. ft.

1. According to the above table, the total gas consumed for the week was MOST NEARLY _____ cubic feet.

   A. 1000   B. 4000   C. 7000   D. 10,000

2. Gas consumption for Tuesday was MOST NEARLY _____ cubic feet.

   A. 500   B. 1000   C. 2000   D. 8000

3. The day on which gas consumption was LOWEST was

   A. Monday   B. Tuesday   C. Wednesday   D. Thursday

Questions 4-6.

DIRECTIONS: Questions 4 through 6 are to be answered ONLY on the basis of the information given below.

A certain job requires 4 men working the number of hours and at the salary rate indicated in the accompanying table.

Name	No. of hours	Salary/hr.
Brown	30	$5.00
Jones	22	$6.50
Walter	40	$3.50
Thomas	25	$5.74

4. According to the above table, the salary received by Thomas on this job is MOST NEARLY

   A. $142.00   B. $142.50   C. $143.00   D. $143.50

5. According to the above table, the man who received the MOST wages chargeable to this job is

   A. Brown   B. Jones   C. Walter   D. Thomas

6. According to the above table, the total amount of wages chargeable to this job is MOST NEARLY

   A. $575.50   B. $572.50   C. $576.50   D. $579.00

KEY (CORRECT ANSWERS)

1. D
2. C
3. A
4. D
5. A
6. C

# TEST 6

Questions 1-20.

DIRECTIONS: Questions 1 through 20 are to be answered ONLY on the basis of the information given in he table below.

LUMBER LIST FOR DOUBLE DESK

Part	No. of Pieces	Thickness In Inches	Width In Inches	Length In Inches
Top panel	6	7/8	10 1/2	48
Edge banding	4	1/4	1 3/4	182
Legs	2	3 1/4	3 1/4	28 5/8
Leg cleats	2	7/8	5 3/4	21
Side and back panels (plywood)	6	1/4	21 3/4	24 7/8
Top and bottom rails	4	3/4	1 5/8	17 3/4
Drawer rails	6	3/4	7/8	17 3/4
Side rails	12	3/4	2 1/4	19 1/4
Drawer slides	16	3/4	2 1/4	18 5/8
Drawer guides	16	3/4	1 1/4	17 3/4
Drawer fronts	8	3/4	5 1/2	17 3/4
Drawer sides	16	3/8	4 3/4	19 3/4
Drawer backs	8	1/2	4 3/4	17 3/8
Drawer bottoms (plywood)	8	1/4	17 3/8	19 1/4

1. The number of pieces used for the legs is

   A. 2 B. 4 C. 6 D. 8

2. The thickness of the drawer sides is

   A. 1/4" B. 3/8" C. 1/2" D. 3/4"

3. The width of the drawer slides is

   A. 7/8" B. 1 5/7" C. 1/2" D. 3/4"

4. The part that has a length of 24 7/8" is the

   A. drawer sides B. legs
   C. side and back panels D. top panel

5. The THICKEST part is the

   A. drawer backs B. edge banding
   C. legs D. side and back panels

6. The part with the SMALLEST width is the

   A. drawer rails B. drawer bottoms
   C. drawer backs D. top panel

7. The parts made of plywood are the _____ and _____.

   A. drawer slides; top and bottom rails
   B. legs; leg cleats
   C. side and back panels; drawer bottoms
   D. top panel; edge banding

8. The part having a length of 17 3/4" and requiring 6 pieces is the

   A. drawer guides
   B. drawer rails
   C. side and back panels
   D. top and bottom rails

9. The number of drawers this desk has is MOST probably

   A. 4   B. 6   C. 8   D. 12

10. The parts with the LONGEST and SHORTEST lengths, respectively, a.re the

    A. drawer guides and drawer fronts
    B. edge banding and top panel
    C. edge banding and drawer backs
    D. top and bottom rails and drawer rails

11. The combined number of pieces needed for the drawer slides and drawer guides is

    A. 32   B. 28   C. 24   D. 22

12. The part that has a width of 4 3/4" and a thickness of 3/8" is the

    A. drawer backs
    B. drawer sides
    C. edge banding
    D. leg cleats

13. The part that has a thickness of 3/4" and a length of 18 5/8" is the

    A. top and bottom rails
    B. drawer fronts
    C. drawer guides
    D. drawer slides

14. The part having a thickness of 3/4" which requires the LEAST number of pieces is the

    A. drawer fronts
    B. drawer rails
    C. legs
    D. top and bottom rails

15. The part having a thickness of 3/4", a width of 2 1/4", and a length of 19 1/4" is the

    A. drawer fronts
    B. drawer sides
    C. drawer slides
    D. side rails

16. The part that is 10 1/2" wide is the

    A. top panel
    B. leg cleats
    C. drawer fronts
    D. drawer bottoms

17. The combined length of the legs and of the side and back panels is

    A. 43 1/2"   B. 47 7/8"   C. 49 5/8"   D. 53 1/2"

18. The part for which 16 pieces are needed and which is 3/4" thick and 1 1/4" wide is the

    A. drawer guides
    B. drawer slides
    C. drawer sides
    D. side and back panels

19. Of the following, the part with the SHORTEST length and SMALLEST width is the

    A. drawer fronts
    B. drawer guides
    C. drawer rails
    D. top and bottom rails

20. The height of this desk is MOST probably

    A. 18 5/8"   B. 24 7/8"   C. 29 1/2"   D. 182"

KEY (CORRECT ANSWERS)

1.	A	11.	A
2.	B	12.	B
3.	C	13.	D
4.	C	14.	D
5.	C	15.	D
6.	A	16.	A
7.	C	17.	D
8.	B	18.	A
9.	C	19.	C
10.	C	20.	C

INTERPRETING STATISTICAL DATA GRAPHS, CHARTS AND TABLES
EXAMINATION SECTION
TEST 1

DIRECTIONS: Each question or incomplete statement is followed by several suggested answers or completions. Select the one that BEST answers the question or completes the statement. *PRINT THE LETTER OF THE CORRECT ANSWER IN THE SPACE AT THE RIGHT.*

Questions 1-4.

DIRECTIONS: Questions 1 through 4 are to be answered on the basis of the chart below which provides information about the current assignments of a group of agents.

Name of Agent	Code No. of Assignment	Date Assigned	Section No.	Name of Supervisor
Estes, Jerome	34-08-A	10/8/18	F0281	H. Landon
Gomez, Margie	34-07-A	10/15/18	F0281	S. Lee
Isaac, John	32-07-B	10/8/18	F0381	R. Puente
Kaplan, Pearl	32-07-A	11/5/18	F0381	R. Puente
Kapler, Peter	34-05-A	10/22/18	F0281	S. Lee
Karell, Peter	42-05-A	11/12/18	F1281	T. Pujol

1. Two of the agents received their current assignments on the same date. This date is

    A. October 8, 2018
    B. October 15, 2018
    C. October 22, 2018
    D. November 12, 2018

1.____

2. Which of the following is Peter Kapler's section number?

    A. 34-05-A   B. 42-05-A   C. F0281   D. F1281

2.____

3. R. Puente is the supervisor for

    A. John Isaac *only*
    B. John Isaac and Pearl Kaplan
    C. John Isaac, Pearl Kaplan, and Peter Kapler
    D. John Isaac, Pearl Kaplan, and Peter Karell

3.____

4. How many of the agents were given their current assignments BEFORE November 1, 2018?

    A. 2   B. 4   C. 5   D. 6

4.____

KEY (CORRECT ANSWERS)

1. A
2. C
3. B
4. B

TEST 2

Questions 1-4.

DIRECTIONS: Questions 1 through 4 are to be answered SOLELY on the basis of the information given below.

NUMBER OF SPECIAL ORDERS PICKED AND PACKED EACH DAY DURING WEEK

Stockman A - Monday 20; Tuesday 20; Wednesday 25; Thursday 30; Friday 30

Stockman B - Monday 25; Tuesday 30; Wednesday 35; Thursday 20; Friday 35

Stockman C - Monday 15; Tuesday 20; Wednesday 25; Thursday 30; Friday 30

Stockman D - Monday 30; Tuesday 35; Wednesday 40; Thursday 35; Friday 40

1. Which stockman picked and packed a total of exactly 120 special orders during the week?
   Stockman

   A. A   B. B   C. C   D. D

2. The stockman who picked and packed the LEAST number of special orders on Thursday is Stockman

   A. A   B. B   C. C   D. D

3. The total number of special orders picked and packed during the week by all four stockmen is

   A. 125   B. 460   C. 560   D. 570

4. By what percentage did the number of orders picked and packed by Stockman C on Friday exceed the number of orders picked and packed by Stockman C on Monday?

   A. 15%   B. 30%   C. 100%   D. 200%

KEY (CORRECT ANSWERS)

1. C
2. B
3. D
4. C

TEST 3

Questions 1-3.

DIRECTIONS: Questions 1 through 3 are to be answered SOLELY on the basis of the information contained in the following chart.

CHART A								
MILEAGE BETWEEN NEW YORK AND POINTS IN NEARBY CONNECTICUT								
	New York	Bridge-port	Dan-bury	Hart-ford	New Haven	New London	Stam-ford	Water-bury
New York	--	61	66	115	80	132	39	91
Bridgeport	61	--	27	54	19	71	22	30
Danbury	66	27	--	57	33	85	31	30
Hartford	115	54	57	--	37	44	76	27
New Haven	80	19	33	37	--	52	41	21
New London	132	71	85	44	52	--	93	62
Stamford	39	22	31	76	41	93		52
Waterbury	91	30	30	27	21	62	52	--

1. According to Chart A, the TOTAL mileage on a continuous trip from New York to Danbury, to Waterbury, to New London, to New York would be _____ miles.

    A. 280   B. 290   C. 316   D. 294

2. According to Chart A, the mileage between New Haven and New London is the same as the mileage between _____ and _____

    A. Danbury; Hartford
    C. Stamford; New Haven
    B. Hartford; New London
    D. Waterbury; Stamford

3. According to Chart A, which of the following pairs of cities are CLOSEST to each other?

    A. Bridgeport and Hartford
    C. Hartford and Danbury
    B. New York and Bridgeport
    D. New Haven and New London

KEY (CORRECT ANSWERS)

1. B
2. D
3. D

TEST 4

Questions 1-6.

DIRECTIONS: Questions 1 through 6 are to be answered SOLELY on the basis of the information given in the following chart.

PERSONNEL SCHEDULE OF ELEVATOR OPERATORS
AS OF DECEMBER 2017

Name	Sex	Month and Year of Birth	Month & Year Entered City Service	Building Assigned	Rate of Pay
Adams, Henry	M	Jan. 1992	March 2013	Municipal	$18,940
Brown, Thomas	M	Apr. 1960	July 1991	Hall of Records	$19,660
Ford, Alice	F	Dec. 1973	Apr. 2003	Municipal	$19,660
Gates, Sidney	M	July 1997	Jan. 2016	Q-12 Storehouse	$17,860
Hill, Irene	F	Oct. 1983	Sept. 1992	Bergen	$19,660
Jones, Jack	M	June 1987	June 2008	Q-12 Storehouse	$19,660
Lewis, Philip	M	Aug. 1995	Oct. 2013	Municipal	$18,580
Roth, William	M	Jan. 1966	Jan. 1985	Q-12 Storehouse	$19,660
Smith, Rose	F	Mar. 1978	July 2005	Hall of Records	$19,660
Wood, Mary	F	Dec. 1994	Feb. 2014	Municipal	$18,580

1. The building which has the MOST male elevator operators assigned to it is

   A. Municipal
   B. Hall of Records
   C. Q-12 Storehouse
   D. Bergen

2. To what building is the female operator with the LOWEST salary assigned?

   A. Municipal
   B. Hall of Records
   C. Q-12 Storehouse
   D. Bergen

3. To what building is the OLDEST male elevator operator with more than 25 years of service assigned?

   A. Municipal
   B. Hall of Records
   C. Q-12 Storehouse
   D. Bergen

4. To what building is the female operator who has been in city service the LONGEST assigned?

   A. Municipal
   B. Hall of Records
   C. Q-12 Storehouse
   D. Bergen

5. The combined wages paid to all the female operators is MOST NEARLY

   A. $78,000   B. $80,000   C. $82,000   D. $84,000

6. The YOUNGEST operator with less than 4 years of city service assigned to the Municipal Building is
 6.____

   A. Adams   B. Gates   C. Lewis   D. Wood

KEY (CORRECT ANSWERS)

1. C
2. A
3. B
4. D
5. A
6. D

TEST 5

Questions 1-5.

DIRECTIONS: Questions 1 through 5 are to be answered on the basis of the information given in the table below.

Date of Water Meter Reading	Water Meter Readings in Cubic Feet				
	Meter 1	Meter 2	Meter 3	Meter 4	Meter 5
Dec. 31, 2013	12,416	88,990	64,312	26,985	30,057
June 30, 2014	23,094	98,806	71,527	27,336	30,057
Dec. 31, 2014	33,011	07,723	79,292	27,848	30,618
June 30, 2015	42,907	16,915	87,208	28,286	31,247
Dec. 31, 2015	52,603	26,456	95,244	28,742	31,740

NOTE: The maximum readings of each of the above five meters is 99,999 cubic feet. Above that reading, the meters start registering from zero.

NOTE: Assume that the maximum water consumption between consecutive readings is less than 100,000 cubic feet.

1. The meter which showed the LOWEST water consumption for the period June 30, 2015 to December 31, 2015 is Meter

   A. 2   B. 3   C. 4   D. 5

2. The amount of water consumed between June 30, 2014 and December 31, 2014 by the consumers metered by Meter 2 is _____ cubic feet.

   A. 7,723   B. 8,917   C. 91,083   D. 107,723

3. The meter which showed the GREATEST water consumption over the time period December 31, 2013 to December 31, 2015 is Meter

   A. 1   B. 2   C. 3   D. 4

4. The meter which showed EXACTLY the same water consumption for 2015 as in 2014 is Meter

   A. 1   B. 2   C. 4   D. 5

5. The meter which shows EXACTLY TWICE as much water consumption in 2015 as compared to the consumption in 2014 is Meter

   A. 1   B. 3   C. 4   D. 5

KEY (CORRECT ANSWERS)

1. C
2. B
3. A
4. B
5. D

TEST 6

Questions 1-5.

DIRECTIONS: Questions 1 through 5 are to be answered SOLELY on the basis of the information given in the table below, which shows the attendance and locker receipts at Pool Y one week.

WEEKLY RECORD AT POOL Y		
DAY	ATTENDANCE	LOCKER RECEIPTS
Monday	200	$300.00
Tuesday	385	577.50
Wednesday	275	412.50
Thursday	330	495.00
Friday	460	690.00
Saturday	500	1,250.00
Sunday	650	1,625.00
Total	?	$5,350.00

1. The TOTAL attendance for the week was

    A. 1,500   B. 1,800   C. 2,500   D. 2,800

2. The GREATEST increase in attendance, from one day to the next, was from _____ to _____.

    A. Monday; Tuesday   B. Tuesday; Wednesday
    C. Friday; Saturday   D. Saturday; Sunday

3. If each person attending on Saturday paid for a locker, the average charge for a locker on Saturday was

    A. $1.00   B. $1.50   C. $2.50   D. $3.50

4. The locker receipts for Saturday were

    A. *less* than four times the lowest receipts for any weekday
    B. *less* than the total of the three lowest weekday receipts
    C. *less* than two times the highest receipts for any weekday
    D. *more* than the combined receipts for any 2 weekdays

5. The SMALLEST increase in attendance, with the comparatively greatest increase in locker receipts, was from _____ to _____

    A. Tuesday; Wednesday   B. Wednesday; Thursday
    C. Thursday; Friday   D. Friday; Saturday

KEY (CORRECT ANSWERS)

1. D
2. A
3. C
4. C
5. D

TEST 7

Questions 1-4.

DIRECTIONS: Questions 1 through 4 are to be answered on the basis of the information given below.

	LISTING OF PAPER FOUND IN STOCKROOM A			
Description	Quantity Ordered by Stock room A (In dozen reams)	Quantity in Stock Before Delivery (In dozen reams)	Cost Per Ream	Location of Stock in Stockroom
8 1/2"x11" Blue	17	5	$1.88	Bin A7
8 1/2"x11" Buff	8	3	$1.86	Bin A7
8 1/2"x11" Green	11	4	$1.90	Bin B4
8 1/2"x11" Pink	10	4	$1.86	Bin B4
8 1/2"x11" White	80	15	$1.72	Bin A8
8 1/2"x13" White	76	12	$2.04	Bin A8
8 1/2"x14" Blue	7	2	$2.38	Bin A7
8 1/2"x14" Buff	7	3	$2.36	Bin A7
8 1/2"x14" Green	5	2	$2.40	Bin B4
8 1/2"x14" Pink	8	4	$2.36	Bin B4
8 1/2"x14" White	110	28	$2.30	Bin A8
8 1/2"x14" Yellow	2	1	$2.46	Bin C6

1. How many reams of 8 1/2" x 13" paper will there be in stock if only one-half of the amount ordered is delivered? _____ reams.

    A. 456 B. 600 C. 912 D. 1,056

2. Suppose all ordered material is delivered.
   The bin that will have the MOST reams of paper is

    A. A7 B. A8 C. B4 D. C6

3. Suppose all ordered material has been delivered.
   What is the APPROXIMATE value of all 8 1/2" x 11" paper which is in Bin B4?

    A. $54 B. $342 C. $396 D. $654

4. How many reams of white paper of all sizes were ordered? _____ reams.

    A. 55 B. 266 C. 660 D. 3,192

Before any of the orders were delivered, the following requests were filled and removed from the stockroom:
2 dozen reams 8 1/2" x 11" Blue; 2 dozen reams 8 1/2" x 11" Green;
7 dozen reams 8 1/2" x 11" White; 5 dozen reams 8 1/2" x 13" White;
1 dozen reams 8 1/2" x 14" Green; 13 dozen reams 8 1/2" x 14" White.
How many reams of paper were left in the stockroom after the above requests were filled?

5._____

A. 30 B. 53 C. 636 D. 996

KEY (CORRECT ANSWERS)

1. B
2. B
3. D
4. D
5. C